# Educating Rita

## WILLY RUSSELL

Guide written by

**Lorna Syred**

First published 1997

Letts Educational
Aldine House
Aldine Place
London W12 8AW
0181 740 2266



**Typeset by** Jordan Publishing Design

**Text design** Jonathan Barnard

**Cover and text illustrations** Ivan Allen



**Acknowledgements**
Extracts from *Educating Rita*, © Willy Russell, are reproduced by kind permission of the publisher, Methuen Drama.

Examination questions reproduced by kind permission of the Midland Examining Group, and London Examinations, a division of Edexcel Foundation.

The answers supplied to the Exam Board questions are solely the responsibility of the author, and are not supplied or approved by the Exam Boards.



**British Library Cataloguing in Publication Data**
A CIP record for this book is available from the British Library

ISBN 1 85758 625 5

Printed and bound in Great Britain
Ashford Colour Press, Gosport, Hampshire

Letts Educational is the trading name of BPP (Letts Educational) Ltd

# Contents

# Plot synopsis

*Educating Rita* is very simple in terms of storyline and structure. It has two Acts which use the same set throughout. There are only two people on stage, although other characters are made vivid through dialogue.

The plot itself is as follows. Rita is a young, working-class hairdresser who has made the difficult decision to break away from the restrictions placed upon her by her family and her community. She has decided to become more educated and culturally aware, and she joins an Open University course on literature. Frank, a disillusioned writer and alcoholic, is her tutor. He is initially unwilling to tutor her, fearing to spoil her essential innocence and honesty. He believes an education will corrupt her.

Rita has to contend with strong opposition from her husband, who resents the way she has changed, and wishes to start a family. When her husband discovers that she has continued to take the pill without his knowledge, he makes her choose between him and her college course. She chooses her course. From this point on she is determined to improve herself. Her trip to summer school is a huge landmark for her. She meets other students who share her passion and interest, and she begins to throw herself into a new way of life. She becomes very absorbed with culture and literature and Frank feels his worst fears for her have been justified.

Rita is made to confront her own superficiality when her flatmate attempts suicide. This makes her realise that high culture, art and literature are not the answers to all of life's problems. Despite this realisation, she chooses to write her exam, and passes well. She returns to Frank, with whom she has quarrelled, to offer an apology and to acknowledge the true worth of her education. Frank himself has been sent away from the college because of his drunken behaviour. He asks Rita if she will join him in Australia, but she avoids answering by reflecting on the many choices available to her now. She tells Frank that there is only one thing she can give him in return for all he has done – a good haircut!

# Who's who in *Educating Rita*

**Rita**

## Rita

Rita is one of only two characters in the play and her development is the focus of the plot. Both the structure and storyline depend on Rita's progression from cocky ignorance through shallow knowledge to, finally, wisdom. The fluidity and progression of the character contrasts sharply with the rather stale and static depiction of Frank, her tutor.

Rita's first entrance is typical of her presentation throughout the play. She enters the room, walks to the desk, goes to hang her coat up, goes over to the picture, back to the desk and then over to look at a bookcase – all within the first few seconds of her arrival. We have the impression of constant motion, of an innate restlessness and curiosity. This idea of movement is heightened by the image of Frank sitting at his desk, as if in the centre of a whirlwind.

The idea of physical restlessness is reflected in Rita's *mental* restlessness: her mind seems to move from thought to thought as swiftly as she moves around the room. Frank later comments on this trait of hers, with some irritation: 'When you come into this room you'll do anything except start work immediately... ' and, 'Don't you ever just walk into a room and sit down?' Despite having an enquiring mind and many ideas about life, Rita lacks discipline of thought and concentration, and as Frank points out to her, 'Possessing a hungry mind is not, in itself, a guarantee of success... ' and, '... if you're going to pass any sort of exam you have to begin to discipline that mind of yours.' This quirky, irreverent and unpolished nature is, of course, the very quality that draws Frank to Rita, and he watches in helpless horror as she becomes more and more dependent on literature, art, high culture and 'intellectuals' to inform her views on life.

Since the action of the play is contained within one setting, and there are only two characters, we learn about

Rita's life and circumstances through her dialogue with Frank. She is a married woman of twenty six who works in a local hairdressers. Her husband's wish for them to start a family has thrown Rita into crisis: she wishes to explore life and herself more before she takes on such a commitment. This need for self-development has led her into deceiving her husband, Denny, who does not know that she is continuing to take the contraceptive pill. It is this deception that really brings about Rita's journey of self-discovery. When Denny realises the real situation, Rita is forced to make a true commitment: she must give herself to Denny and start a family, or continue to pursue her studies. She chooses to study.

How far do you agree with the wisdom of Rita's choice? Frank, as Rita's tutor, has reservations: 'When art and literature take the place of life itself, perhaps it's time to…'; 'We should really talk about you and Denny, my dear.' Do you, like Frank, feel that Rita places too little value upon what she has already and too much upon something that is divorced from life itself? Or is she right to follow her need to know and understand more before starting a family? 'I know he's right. But I couldn't betray meself.' Perhaps, like most issues in life, the truth lies somewhere between the two, and perhaps it is this truth that Rita stumbles across towards the end of the play: 'I was so hungry. I wanted it all so much that I didn't want it to be questioned.' You will need to decide for yourself how successful Rita's 'education' has been, and to what extent it has changed her life for the better.

## Frank

Frank remains an effective contrast to Rita throughout the play. Whilst Rita is constantly discovering and developing, Frank remains static. Any sense of movement or progression of this character is one of a downward slide: he continues to drink, his relationship with his girlfriend deteriorates and, by the end of the play, he has lost his position in the University. There is some sense of hope in his arrival at rock-bottom, though: he is being sent to a country 'that's just beginning.' Both he and Rita seem about to start their lives anew at the play's ending.

Frank is often presented as sedentary, sitting at his desk while Rita paces restlessly around him. The two main exceptions to this are Act 2 Scene 3 when he is exhilarated by his own drunken, boorish behaviour, and the final scene, when he has been forced into having to pack up and go. In both of these scenes his physical movement carries a sense of destruction. His drunken antics in Act 2 Scene 3 are the result of the students' complaints, and the last scene shows his final dismissal.

The study where we watch Frank and Rita's relationship unfold is heavily symbolic of Frank himself. The faulty door handle is a device for humour, but also implies the idea of Frank having almost barricaded himself in or, at least, of visitors being rather a rarity. When Rita sweeps in, he is forced to look around him: he admits to not having looked at the picture on his wall for 'about ten years', and when Rita points out his window he says, 'I don't often consider it actually.' Rita's wide-eyed sense of awe of everything he takes for granted provides some freshness and stimulation for Frank. As he puts it, Rita is 'the first breath of fresh air that's been in this room for years.'

Frank's study later becomes representative of the stifling influence that Rita feels Frank has become. When Rita returns from summer school, bursting with enthusiasm and new ideas, she feels the need to escape from the claustrophobic room. She discovers that the window, like the door, is stuck closed. Frank says 'I'm not surprised, my dear. It hasn't been opened for generations.' Rita's rather laughable attempt at figurative speech – 'A room is like a plant' – is perhaps suggestive of her need to grow and expand, rather than be confined by Frank. She has outgrown the study, and feels the need to escape from it, in the same way that she feels the need to escape from Frank. Even Frank acknowledges the stifling atmosphere he creates: 'Well I certainly don't want to see you stuck in a room like this for the rest of your life.'

Despite Frank's presentation as a still character who has taken root in his study, Frank does have a life away from the University and Rita, and we are reminded of this from time to time. He has an ex-wife, a girlfriend, a comfortable middle-class life and has enjoyed some small success as a poet. He seems to place little value on these things however.

This is an attitude which increasingly incenses Rita because she has struggled so hard for just a little of what he has: 'It's little to you who squanders every opportunity and mocks and takes it for granted.'

In some ways, Frank is a man bent on self-destruction. He is an alcoholic, with no desire to reform and we, with Rita, watch as he allows his life to disintegrate. How far does his character arouse your pity? Can you feel sympathy for his obvious boredom with his circumstances? The contrast between the two is followed through to the end: Rita actively intervenes to stop the circumstances of her life from being in control; Frank more or less surrenders himself to the circumstances of his life.

# Themes and images in *Educating Rita*

**Personal relationships**

## Personal relationships

*Educating Rita* closely examines the relationship between teacher and pupil, and in doing so, reveals the personal element in this kind of relationship. Rita and Frank respond to each other on a personal level right from the beginning of their acquaintance. After an impersonal start – 'Now, you are?' – clearly typical of how he treats his other students, Frank treats her in a very 'un-teacherly' manner: 'Do you know, I think you're the first breath of fresh air that's been in this room for years.' He even feels that she is worth more than he has to offer as a teacher and tells her to find another tutor.

Rita, too, demands more from Frank than a conventional student-teacher relationship. She 'tests' him, finding out whether he is too prudish to smoke or swear. She initially likes the fact that he shamelessly drinks whilst at work. For Rita, at first, the personal element is very important: 'If I'd got some other tutor I wouldn't have stayed.' Towards the end of the play, however, Frank's unconventional, familiar behaviour has become a source of irritation to her. She has become concerned only with literature and with her progress on her course. This is the outcome that Frank has foreseen and dreaded.

At the end of the play, Rita tells Frank that she has only taken from him, never given. In fact, the dynamic of the relationship between the two is not as simple as this. Rita starts off being dependent on Frank, and then reaches a stage where she needs him less and feels an urge to break away. Frank, conversely, seems to develop a need for Rita and feels betrayed when she no longer turns to him: 'It struck me that there was a time when you told me everything.' Why does Frank develop this need? What is it that Rita has 'given' him? Do you think that Frank was right to allow the relationship to develop into an emotional/personal one? Could it have been avoided?

One interpretation of their relationship is that it is a changing balance of power. This is certainly how Rita views it, before she realises what Frank has done for her: 'What's up, Frank, don't y' like me now that the little girl's grown up, now that y' can no longer bounce me on daddy's knee an' watch me stare back in wonder at everything he has to say?' Frank is initially able to impress Rita, and to manipulate her ideas and views on life and literature. Later, as she gathers strength and becomes exposed to other influences (summer school, Trish, other students) she begins to question his ideas and judgements. This changes the balance of power in the relationship because Rita's real need for Frank and his tutorials is no longer present. It appears to be Frank who is left with a need for the relationship to continue, in its old form: 'You really don't have to put in the odd appearance out of sentimentality... I'd rather you spared me that.' How far do you agree with this idea? Perhaps all relationships are power relationships in some way. Rita compares her relationship with Frank to a parental one: how do parents feel when children begin to need them less and finally go away? Do you think this compares well with Frank's situation? Have you ever been in a situation where someone's support and advice, once valuable, became cumbersome? Perhaps you, like Rita, failed to acknowledge just how much that person had given you when you needed them. Why was it so easy to forget?

It might be helpful, at this point, to examine the other personal relationships in the play: Frank and Julia, and Rita and Denny. Our information about these people comes solely through the dialogue between Rita and Frank. Julia is Frank's girlfriend. We realise right from the start of the play that she must have a great deal of patience and tolerance to stay with Frank. What kind of relationship do you think they have? It might be worth noting that Frank tells us that she is an 'ex-student' and that she admires him 'tremendously.' How does this tie in with what we already know about Frank? Why might it be important that she was once his student? And why is she so willing to put up with him? What does she get out of the relationship?

Frank seems to have a passive attitude towards the relationship, supporting his presentation as a rather static character. It is Julia who 'took him on', implying that he had no active role in forming their relationship. It is also Julia who 'left' during the holiday to France, and then returns afterwards. His description of her return is also passive: 'Perfect. I get the feeling we shall stay together forever…' as if he has no part to play in the well-being of their relationship or in his choice of partner – it is just something that 'happens' to him. This presentation of his relationship with Julia seems to be in keeping with his overall characterisation.

Denny is Rita's husband. He blames Rita's determination to be educated for the breakdown of their relationship, even going to the extreme of burning her books. He has little faith in the value of an education, feeling content with the life he already leads. How far do you find yourself sympathising with Denny? He clearly loves family life, and we are given the impression that he and Rita have shared happier days. Is it fair of Rita to suddenly declare she wants more? Rather like Frank, Denny does not understand that Rita needs space to grow and develop. Their relationship, like her relationship with Frank, has become a restricting one. She compares her relationship with Denny to her relationship with Frank, not realising that this, too, will become suffocating as she outgrows it: 'I've tried to explain to him how you give me room to breathe. Y' just, like feed me without expectin' anythin' in return.'

Denny and Julia are different from each other in many ways: they are from opposite ends of the social spectrum; Julia is long-suffering and patient, while Denny is volatile and demanding. They are similar in that they both appear to want to have some control over their partners. Julia's control is that of the saviour seeking to make herself needed and worthy of gratitude; Denny's control is more direct and forceful, seeking to make Rita share his own values and lifestyle. Perhaps Rita and Frank's private relationships are as much to do with control and power as their relationship with each other. *Educating Rita* is a close-up look at one particular relationship which makes us question the nature of relationships in general.

**Class, culture and education**

## Class, culture and education

Frank and Rita come from very different English cultures and backgrounds. Neither is content with the culture they exist in and both, to some extent, envy the other. At the start of the play, both seem to see the other as being more 'free' than they are themselves.

Rita comes from a working-class background, somewhere in the North of England. Willy Russell himself is from Liverpool, and this is where the film of the play is set. Rita has a lot to say about the culture and community she has been brought up in. She sees it as a stranglehold, holding her back from realising her true potential and from understanding more about life. She paints a bleak picture of her society, even though it is later presented as a warm and caring one. She claims that it is a society without culture: 'I just see everyone pissed or on the Valium, tryin' to get from one day to the next.' She also makes a lucid attack on the way that the less educated classes are encouraged to become consumers in order to cover up what is really missing. 'The Unions tell them to go out an' get more money an' ITV an' the papers tell them what to spend it on so the disease is always covered up.' Rita appears to be seeking an education and a culture in the same way that people seek a religion or love. She is seeking something that will give meaning to her life and fulfil her. Do you think this is too much to ask of an education? Why is it so hard for Rita to reconcile her working-class background with being educated? Why is Denny so set against it?

When Rita says that the working classes 'have no culture', Frank contradicts her. In a way, he is right because images of the cultures they both inhabit are presented through their conversations with each other. Rita refers to many of the popular cultural icons and images of the '70s and '80s: *Charlie's Angels*, the 'Flora man', Harold Robbins. Frank's cultural framework is that of literature and academia: Oscar Wilde, Mary Shelley, T. S. Eliot. The result, shown most clearly in Act 1 Scene 1, is that they are almost speaking in a different language to each other. In turn, you may find that it is hard to recognise any of the references: Frank's references are rather obscure for school students, and Rita's popular cultural references may no longer hold significance. You will have developed your own 'culture' which you share with others of the same social grouping. Do you think the cultural gap which exists between Frank and Rita is realistic? Or do you think it is possible to have an understanding of 'high' culture and of popular culture?

It is worth remembering that *Educating Rita* was first performed in 1980. Do you think much has changed, nearly two decades on? Do you think that education is more widely available to more people? Think about your own social background. Are you encouraged to learn and experience 'high' culture, or would this be considered socially unacceptable? How acceptable is it to work hard and do well at school? It is important to your understanding of the play that you consider the social issues in relation to yourself and the times you live in. Have things moved on? Are you aware of class and cultural divides in the same way that Rita was made to be? How many students in your class at school have been to the theatre recently, and how many would not consider going? *Educating Rita* was a relevant and eloquent comment on the social and class structure of the country at the time it was written. It is for you, as members of society two decades on, to decide whether it is still valid today.

**Literature**

## Literature

Rita has chosen to study Literature in order to become more educated and culturally aware. Her understanding of what is and isn't good 'literature' develops from a total inability to discriminate between good and bad fiction to a rather 'over-the-top' snobbishness about what is worthwhile. Several questions are raised around this idea of 'literature'. Rita arrives at with no understanding of the difference between literature and popular fiction. When she challenges Frank about the difference between the two, the best he can come up with is 'I -erm -erm – one's always known really.' Frank's own poetry is literature, and he views it with contempt, unable to bring himself to write any more: 'Poets shouldn't believe in literature.' What he seems to mean by this is that he spent too long trying to make his poetry belong to an elite 'high' culture, rather than just being sincere, honest and true to himself in his writing. He has come to value simplicity and passion above a 'clever pyrotechnical pile of self-conscious allusion', which is how he describes his work. Rita, with her passionate enthusiasm and straightforward outlook, unconsciously embodies his ideas on this subject, and this is why he is drawn to her. It is also why he is so reluctant to take on the task of teaching her to objectively appreciate 'real' literature.

Russell himself asserts something similar to Frank's views in the preface of his play in the Methuen edition. He believes that a play is a failure unless it is able to be understood as it stands: there should be no need to go away and look up references or find out background information in order to appreciate it. This is certainly true of *Educating Rita* – it is accessible to anyone with a small knowledge of English life and education; its humour is easy to find, and the ideas and issues are clear after a little thought. There are times, though, when Russell seems to make some use of 'allusion' – subtle reference to other works of art or literature, which help to unlock the writer's ideas. Rita struggles to understand the ideas in *Howards End*, a novel by E. M. Forster. The novel contains several strands which seem relevant to *Educating Rita*. Firstly, the story deals with the misfortune of a poor clerk, Leonard Bast, who is determined to improve himself by a devotion to books, art and culture. These things seem to have more importance than his real life. Leonard dies, significantly, buried under a pile of books. His aspirations, and his association with the highly cultured Schlegel sisters are partly the cause of his downfall.

The full version of Forster's phrase that Rita struggles with is: 'Only connect the prose and the passion and human love will be seen at its height.' It is a plea for people to reconcile opposites, both between people and within themselves. Howards End portrays conflicting outlooks on life: practical, businesslike, conservative; passionate, romantic, impulsive. The novel draws to its conclusion when the two kinds of natures are able to coexist in harmony. Rita also learns to reconcile the two different sides of her nature. She eventually acknowledges that the world that she has longed to belong to does not have any automatic claims to superiority over other ways of life.

Another literary reference is to *Macbeth*, a tragedy by Shakespeare. Frank explains to Rita the real definition of tragedy, and we can see that it rather subtly foreshadows Frank's own feelings about Rita's 'education' and, perhaps, even himself: 'Erm- it's that flaw which forces him to take the inevitable steps towards his own doom. You see?' What does he see as 'inevitable' about Rita and her lust for an education? Does Frank have a 'flaw' which may cause his downfall? Who tries to warn him, and why does it have no effect? Whose tragedy is it, Frank's or Rita's?

Finally, Frank directly compares his tutorship of Rita with Dr Frankenstein's creation of a monster over whom he has no control, and who turns viciously against him. Is this a fair comparison? Or has Frank, like Macbeth 'brought it on himself'?

*Educating Rita* explores and questions the value of literature. It rejects some snobbish attitudes surrounding it, but accepts its worth in provoking us to consider some of the important issues in life – much like the play itself.

**Character development**

## Character development

We have discussed some aspects of character development in detail in other sections of this guide (see 'Rita' and 'Frank' in *Who's who in Educating Rita*, and 'Personal relationships' earlier in this section). We have seen how, in some ways, *Educating Rita* is a study of the development of a relationship and of the characters involved. Rita consciously sets out to 'develop' her mind and lifestyle and we, with Frank, watch the results of her quest unfold. There is some dramatic irony as we begin to learn more about the characters than they know about themselves. We can see that Frank is driving Rita away with his alcoholism and overt sentimentality, and we can see that Rita is using her education to a shallow and superficial end. Both characters, at least initially, are unaware of what they are doing to themselves, despite each one trying to warn the other. Much of this has been dealt with above, but it is worth taking a separate look at how this development is presented to the audience.

Frank and Rita are both 'developed' or 'rounded' characters, even before Rita starts to learn and change. They both reveal the circumstances of their background and they are supplied with clear motivation for their actions. Frank, for example, is provided with a motive for his disillusionment and need to drink: he has suffered a broken marriage, which was obviously based on youthful romantic notions and ideals: 'One day my wife pointed out to me that... my output as a poet had dealt exclusively with the period in which we – discovered each other.'

This 'roundness' of characterisation makes it possible for us to believe fully in the characters and to accept the changes that they undergo. For example, Rita's successful change into an educated woman takes place in a relatively short space of time (the changing of the seasons indicates approximately one year). How credible would this be if we hadn't known the reasons driving her on to become educated? Or if we hadn't been presented with someone of innate intelligence who was a keen reader before she met Frank? We can see that Frank doesn't perform any miracles with Rita; he just teaches her the skills she needs, and provides her with knowledge. Frank's drunken finale in which he 'buggers the Bursar' in a 'metaphorical' sense is carefully built up in the preceding scenes, so that his exile to Australia is a logical outcome of his behaviour. Even the unexpected attempted suicide of Rita's flatmate, Trish, is cleverly prepared for beforehand with much use of dramatic irony: in Rita's eyes, Trish is 'dead unpretentious', but we are allowed to suspect that she is probably just the opposite: 'As Trish says there is not a lot of point discussing beautiful literature in an ugly voice.' We are left feeling that we know more about Trish than Rita does, simply through what she says about her.

Much of Rita's development as a character is presented to us through her speech. She never really drops her colloquial accent, (except for those few minutes at the beginning of Act 2 Scene 2), but she does become more confident in asserting her views, and in using the language of literature. We see her first attempts at this in Act 2 Scene 1: 'Well any analogy will break down eventually.' She is more convincing in Act 2 Scene 3 when she challenges Frank's interpretation of *The Blossom*: 'It becomes a more rewarding poem when you see that it works on a number of levels.' This is when she really begins to question Frank's authority, and yet fails to question the authority of her other influences.

There are many visual clues, also, to Rita's development. She is depicted as less restless and fidgety in Act 2. Her entrances are quite different from those of Act 1: they are quieter, and she is more inclined to simply walk in and sit down, or go to the desk. On one occasion she is in the room already, reading a book. Her clothes undergo a change of style when she gets back from summer school.

Her last gesture towards Frank takes us full circle to where she started from: she gives Frank a haircut. It is as if it is an acknowledgement of the usefulness of the skills she already had, instead of her previous dismissal of them.

Significantly, much of Rita's development as a character takes place away from Frank and his study. Frank provides Rita with her education, but it is other people who provide her with many of her views on life and literature: Trish, other students, people she meets at summer school. This reinforces the point Rita makes towards the end of the play: 'You think I just ended up with a load of quotes and empty phrases; an' I did. But that wasn't your doin'. I was so hungry.' Frank has provided her with her education, it is up to Rita to use it wisely. At the play's close she has chosen to do this.

**Freedom and choice**

## Freedom and choice

*Educating Rita* offers no easy answers to the issues of class and education. It does, however, offer some solutions for Rita, who has been looking for a way out of her unfulfilled life. The play may seem to send out ambiguous messages about education: it appears to be almost the ruin of Rita, and Frank is depicted as almost regretting his own academic education. The final message of the play, however, is that education is not an end it itself, as Rita sees it, but something which gives people power over their own lives. It gives Rita the freedom and choice that she has been seeking, but in a very different way to the one she had anticipated. It is not necessarily the key to a new lifestyle and self-discovery, but it preserves the freedom of the individual. Rita's emphatic 'I'll make a decision, I'll choose' demonstrates to us that she has finally realised the true value of her education. It has not bought her into a 'better' culture, but has given her the freedom to choose the direction her life will take.

## Examiner's tips

The **Examiner's tips** found throughout the **Text commentary** and **Exam and coursework practice** sections highlight key points in the text, provide advice on avoiding common errors and offer useful hints on thoroughly preparing yourself for coursework and examination essays on this play.

# Text commentary

## Act 1 Scene 1

*The scene opens on Frank's office and the action remains there throughout. It is a typical academic's study, with walls 'lined with books.' Significant features are the 'large bay window', and a print of a nude religious scene on the wall.*

*Frank, a lecturer in English Literature, is frantically trying to find his hidden alcohol, which he has stowed away amongst his books. The telephone rings, and he is heard explaining to someone – presumably a wife or girlfriend – that he will be late for dinner. It is also made clear to us that he is an alcoholic.*

*Rita, his Open University student, arrives after struggling with the door handle to his room. Frank is initially taken aback by her fresh, irreverent approach, but is then pleased and amused.*

*Frank discovers that Rita (whose real name is Susan) is a ladies' hairdresser. Her husband wants her to have a baby, but she feels discontented with her place in life and wishes to 'discover' herself first.*

*Frank, although enchanted by her, tells her she must find another teacher. He feels that she wants, and deserves, more than he can offer. He is also reluctant to change her and says that there is nothing he can teach her. Rita at first acquiesces and leaves. After a moment she comes back in, demanding that Frank be her tutor. She announces that she will return for her lesson next week, and Frank is left with no choice.*

### 'Yes?... of course I'm still here... Because I've got this Open University woman coming, haven't I?...'

Frank's phone call is a device to reveal essential information to the audience.

It is, in a way, a narrative device. This is a play which is rooted in reality and which simply presents a human drama to the audience. A monologue from Frank, or the use of a narrator figure would appear too contrived. We, the audience, are invited to observe the interaction between the characters, and to sympathise with them, but we are never addressed or acknowledged by them. All information is given through dialogue, action and visual clues. Compare this technique to other plays you might have seen or read. What difference does it make to have a character using soliloquy, or a narrator addressing the audience?

From Frank's first speech we learn that he has taken on an Open University student in order to pay for his drinking habit. The caller is obviously annoyed at Frank's 'determination' to go to the pub afterwards. Clearly, this person – who is referred to as 'darling' – has a lot to put up with! We also learn that he is not looking forward to his Open University tutorial. Our initial impression of Frank is formed here: he is witty and likeable, but decadent, irresponsible and cynical.

### 'I'm comin' in, aren't I? It's that stupid bleedin' handle on the door. You wanna get it fixed!'

Rita

This is Rita's first entrance. Her breezy, down-to-earth manner is in direct contrast to the jaded and rather contrived tone of Frank's speech to his girlfriend. As you get further into the play, watch for changes of tone and manner in both of the characters.

Your examiner may want to know that you understand the difference between Standard English and dialectical speech. Examine Rita's language and decide whether she uses grammar in Standard English format. Remember that use of slang and the way you pronounce your words (accent) does not affect the Standard English dialect. Standard English is when words are placed in a particular, accepted order that can be universally understood. Is Rita's dialect different from Standard English, or does she just use a more colloquial turn of phrase to Frank, and a different accent?

### 'It's very erotic.' *Rita*
### 'Actually I don't think I've looked at it for about ten years, but yes, I suppose it is.' *Frank*

Rita

Frank

Rita is referring to a picture of a nude religious scene, hung on Frank's wall. It is a minor incident, but it highlights the difference between Rita's freshness and Frank's weary approach to life. Frank takes a lot for granted, whereas Rita is open and responsive to new things. Rita's comments may well be naive and uneducated, but she is by no means dull or stupid. The incident also foreshadows the way that Rita will make Frank see things in a different way.

The beginning of the play is very important for setting the scene for the rest of the play. For a discussion on how successful the author has been at introducing the characters and themes of the play see question 1 of the example exam questions on page 49.

### 'Howards End?'

Willy Russell writes in his introduction to the Methuen collection of his plays that 'if you need more information than that contained within the plays then the plays are failures… ' and this is a notion that is echoed within *Educating Rita*. Whilst the play is indeed complete in itself, it might also be helpful to know something about the literature that Rita is trying to understand. *Howards End*, by E. M. Forster, is the first novel that Rita studies with Frank. Part of the story is about a young man who is poor, and not highly educated, but seeks to become literate and cultured, like the two young sisters he meets. He holds art and literature to be the most worthy pursuits in life. The two refined and wealthy sisters inadvertently – and through their own ignorance – cause him a great deal of trouble. Finally, and symbolically, when he dies a heavy shelf of books falls on him. As you progress through the text, ask yourself how this story might connect with the two characters in Willy Russell's play.

Literature

### 'It's not their fault; they can't help it. (*She goes to the window and looks out*) But sometimes I hate them. God, what's it like to be free?'

Rita is in awe of the 'educated classes' and credits them with a wisdom and insight that is unavailable to people of her class. She believes that reading and studying will, in itself, give her freedom. The window that Rita looks out of represents the freedom and opportunity that she feels has escaped her. She asks the question of Frank, who she sees as not being trapped in a community or culture he dislikes. As you read on, see whether you agree with this.

Freedom and choice

### 'You're a ladies' hairdresser?'

A biographical point. Russell was a hairdresser, eventually owning his own salon. Like Rita, on slack days he would pursue his real ambition – in his case this was writing. Russell, too, waited some time before becoming a student and pursuing his real ambitions.

### 'Far-rah Fawcett Majors. Y' know, she used to be with *Charlie's Angels*.'

This is one of many comments which humorously show us the wide gap in culture between the two characters. Frank has never heard of this popular television programme, leading Rita to think that he is a 'Flora' man. Unfortunately, Frank has never heard of this reference either! The two have very different frames of cultural reference, almost as if they lived in

Class, culture and education

different countries. Notice that many of Rita's references are from the television, and Frank's are literary.

An interesting point is that you, too, may have a different cultural framework because you may not recognise some of the references to the popular culture of the time. This play was first performed in 1980, when most people would have been familiar with the American detective series *Charlie's Angels*. The show featured three female detectives, all of whom had a style which was imitated by women at the time. Farrah Fawcett Majors had very full, long, blonde hair, which was lifted back from her face, a style that was popular in the '80s. Rita's term 'Flora man' is a reference to an advert for Flora margarine, which claimed that the man who ate it was generally healthier and more refined than other men. So, again, despite Russell's belief that a play should be understood on its owns terms, you may need a bit of help if you were not around at the time of the play's setting.

The examiner will be looking to see that you have a knowledge of the play's context. This will include some knowledge of its cultural setting. Research for this should not be too hard – you could just talk to older relatives about what life was like in the '80s!

### 'I've been realizin' for ages that I was, y' know' slightly out of step.'

We learn about Rita's background in a more direct way here. She feels trapped in her own community and culture and is desperate to find out about herself before she starts a family. In telling Frank this personal information she also lets us know that the course is a brave and difficult step for her. We learn that her need to educate herself is putting a strain on her relationship with her husband.

Class, culture and education

### 'Everything I know – and you must listen to this – is that I know absolutely nothing.'

There is, here, an introduction to the idea of some education being shallow or corruptive. Frank feels that his knowledge of literature and high culture have given him nothing of any value. He takes for granted – or even despises – the things that Rita is so desperately looking for.

Class, culture and education

## Act 1 Scene 2

*Rita returns for her tutorial. She has brought an oil can with her to fix Frank's door for him. When she enters, she notices that Frank has not been drinking. She spends a long time talking to Frank before getting round to doing any work, and we learn a bit more about her motivation for taking the course. Frank hands back her assignment on Rubyfruit Jungle and tells her that she needs to be more objective in her approach to literature. Despite Frank's attempts to get Rita's mind onto her work, she is more interested in finding out about Frank himself.*

### 'You've not been drinking, have y'?'

Rita notices that Frank is not drunk this time and wonders if it is to do with her remarks about it at the last tutorial. Frank laughs at this, and Rita hastily denies that she has an interest in reforming him and changes the subject. What do you make of this? Is there some way in which Rita may have influenced him? Do you believe that she does not want to change him in some way?

**Personal relationships**

### 'I love that lawn down there. When it's summer, do they sit on it?'

Rita has walked over to the bay window which seems to represent a view of the life she would like to have had. She associates it with freedom and opportunity. She speaks wistfully of the students sitting on the grass outside, discussing their studies, as if theirs is the ideal existence. How real is this? What do you think of this notion? Can you foresee what lessons Rita really has to learn? *Educating Rita* is by no means an onslaught against education, but the play urges us to see its true value, and to combine our knowledge with wisdom.

**Class, culture and education**

### 'Cos it's easy... it doesn't upset anyone around y'. Like cos they don't want y' to change.'

We have another insight into Rita's background and the huge decision she has had to make to change her life. She has been swept along by her lifestyle, knowing that if she attempted to achieve something more she would upset the people around her. For a long time she did nothing because it is easier not to think about it.

**Rita**

It is difficult to be different from friends and family: everyone wants and needs to be accepted by the people around them. Rita's dilemma is a common one, however, and one that you might recognise. Have you ever found yourself in a situation where you had to break away from friends or family in order to please yourself? How did they respond?

Russell echoes this theme in his other plays. In *Stags and Hens* the main character, Linda, manages to tear herself away from her community just before she marries into it. She says, 'But it's like, honest, it's like I'm getting married to a town.' *Blood Brothers* is about the difference in fortune of two brothers who are brought up in very different cultures and classes. Culture and community can be an enrichment to life, but also, sometimes, a trap.

## 'Well. You must try to remember that criticism is purely objective. It should be approached almost as a science.'

This is Frank's rather stuffy response to Rita's essay on *Rubyfruit Jungle*. Rita responds honestly to the literature she has read, and yet this is not what is required of her for her examination. What do you think of Frank's statement that 'criticism is purely objective.' Do you think it is possible for any response to literature to be purely objective? Is this how you approach the literature you read? What do you think we are supposed to make of this statement?

**Literature**

The examiner will be looking for your ability to distinguish between the opinions of the author and the opinions of the characters. How far do you think Russell agrees with Frank's outlook on life and literature? It will be hard to work this out until after you have finished the play.

## 'Are you married?'

Rita's undisciplined mind and determination to wander off the subject gives us an opportunity to find out more about Frank. We discover that he has been married, but is now separated. More depth is added to his character when we suspect that he must once have been idealistic and passionate about literature – and about his wife, who inspired his poetry. This revelation lends a poignancy to his cynical, self-deprecating comments.

Frank

## 'I wish I could talk like that. It's brilliant.'

We see here how easily impressed Rita is by Frank's eloquence and education. He is a witty, intelligent man, but in this instance he hasn't said anything devastatingly clever. Watch to see how Rita's judgement of Frank changes as the play progresses. At present she is unable to criticise Frank, but later she will be able to form a more impartial opinion of him.

**Character development**

## 'Right now there's a thousand things I'd rather do than teach; most of them with you, young lady... '

Frank, too, admires Rita for her freshness and honesty. Their admiration is mutual because they both believe the other to have something that they

Personal relationships

themselves lack. It is easy to read some sexual innuendo into some of Frank's comments to Rita, but the relationship never really develops in this way. Still, see if you think there is any more evidence of sexual attraction on either side as you work your way through the play.

## Act 1 Scene 3

*Rita arrives for another tutorial. She has written an essay on the text* Howards End. *She has used unsuitable reference material for her essay (a novel by Harold Robbins), but it transpires that she has actually been doing a lot of reading in the quiet period at the shop. Frank tries to explain to her the difference between good literature and pulp fiction.*

### 'But how d' y' work it out if y' don't know? See that's what I've got to learn, isn't it? I'm dead ignorant y' know.'

Personal relationships

Literature

Notice, in this scene, how readily Rita accepts Frank's criticism and advice and how, despite her initial feistiness, she acknowledges her limitations. Keep an eye on how and when this changes as the play develops.

Do you agree that some books are more 'worthy' than others? Do you agree with Frank or, like Rita, are you unable to tell the difference? Perhaps you could have a go at answering Rita's question better than Frank does. How do you tell whether a book is 'literature,' or not?

### 'Aha. You mean it's all right to go out an' have a bit of slap and tickle with the lads as long as you don't go home and tell your mum?'

Rita is quick to draw comparisons and make connections between different things – qualities needed by the student of literature. She responds quickly to every idea that Frank gives her. We see nothing of stupidity and slowness in Rita; in fact, she is bright, thoughtful and observant. The fact that she is 'ignorant' comes simply from a poor education. Perhaps you can think of many well educated people who are 'ignorant'? Do you think it is the right word to describe Rita?

Rita

The character of Rita presents a real challenge for a good actress. What do you think of Julie Walters' interpretation of her in the film version? See the example coursework question on page 55 for some ideas on character presentation on stage.

## Act 1 Scene 4

*Rita is having trouble with her* Howards End *essay: she cannot understand the meaning behind Forster's phrase 'Only connect... '*

*She has handed in a one line essay on* Peer Gynt*, which Frank insists she redoes. Before Rita settles down to the work she explains to Frank that, like* Peer Gynt*, the people in her community need to find a meaning to their lives. She also tells him that her husband tried to stop her coming to the tutorial that night. During this conversation, Frank is able to point out to her the meaning of 'Only connect...'. Eventually Rita begins her essay, but looks up a moment later to hand it to him. The finished product is all of two sentences long.*

### 'He's got me licked, I don't know what he's on about, 'Only connect, only connect', it's just bleedin' borin'. It's no good, I just can't understand.'

Rita is referring to *Howards End*, the novel she has been struggling with since the beginning of the course. The full quotation is 'Only connect the prose and the passion and human love will be seen at its height.' One of Forster's main concerns as a novelist was the lack of 'connection' between different kinds of people and within people themselves. In *Howards End*, there are two contrasting families: the business orientated, money loving Wilcoxes and the artistic, emotional Schlegel sisters. Margaret Schlegel manages to link the two different sides of human nature when she marries Henry Wilcox. She shows, gradually, that each is needed by the other, despite her sister's outrage at the relationship. *Educating Rita* is also about making these kinds of connections. Rita is trying to connect her world with the world of culture and literature; she has been making connections between literature and life; Frank and Rita's relationship works because each values the other for the way they are. The phrase that Rita cannot understand is about bringing together completely different values and ideas so that they work well. This, of course, is precisely what Rita has been trying to do.

Literature

### 'Y' daren't say that round our way, like, cos they're proud. They'll tell you they've got culture as they sit there drinkin' their keg beer out of plastic glasses.'

Rita explains her disillusionment with her working-class community and with what she see as the 'myth' of culture they are led to believe in. She believes that

Class, culture and education

people like her and her family are led to believe that money and material goods are the answer to the general discontent they all feel. This message, however, is sent out to them by some of the very people who are trying to make money out of them. She sees it as a vicious circle which takes a lot of strength and determination to break away from. She is looking for a way to enrich her life which has nothing to do with money.

Do you agree with Rita's ideas about culture and the working classes? Do you think she will find what she is looking for? Rita speaks of her search for a 'meanin' to life' almost in the same way as someone who is searching for a religion. Can you understand why it is so important to her to become educated and to better understand the world around her? What do you think it is that she really wants from life? Remember her question to Frank as she gazed out of his bay window at their first meeting.

## 'Denny tried to stop me coming tonight.'

We learn more about Rita's relationship with her husband here, and about

Personal relationships

how it has become restrictive and oppressive rather than an equal partnership. Despite Rita's aggressive choice of language – 'stop me' – Denny is no tyrant. He is simply trying to keep their relationship together on the same terms as when they married each other. He is allowing no room for growth or change. This brings home to us just how big a step Rita is taking by doing her course. By changing herself she is also likely to change her relationship with her husband, her family and the world around her. For Rita, getting an education means a whole lot more than simply passing an examination so that she can get a better job, or more money.

Freedom and choice

Think about the reasons you have for studying this text now. Are you learning literature just to pass an exam, or do you hope that your education will have a far greater impact than this?

## 'I could have told you; but you'll have a much better understanding of something if you discover it in your own terms.'

Frank points us towards an important truth here. We can be taught everything

Class, culture and education

there is to know about something, and yet we do not achieve true understanding until we discover it for ourselves. How does Frank's observation tie in with his own opinion of his teaching in Scene 1? And, more importantly, how does it tie in with Rita's thoughts on her education at the end of the play? As you read on, look for the moment when she truly discovers things 'in her own terms.'

### '... he wrote the play as a play for voices, never intending it to go on in a theatre.'

Rita

Rita's 'extended' answer to her *Peer Gynt* question is seemingly flippant and highly unsuitable for an examination, left as it is. There is an underlying intelligence in what she says, however, that is based on common sense and rational thought. It is becoming clearer and clearer that Frank's job in teaching Rita is not one of transforming an idiot into an intellectual, but of nurturing and cultivating the quality of thought that is already there.

Are there any ways in which the phrase 'a play for voices' could apply to *Educating Rita*? In what ways do dialogue, dialect and accent take precedence over some theatrical conventions? How much does the play's humour rest on visual prop? If you have watched the film of the play, to what extent did the director have to change things to make it suitable for this medium?

## Self-test Questions Act 1 Scenes 1–4

**Uncover the plot**

Delete two of the three alternatives given to find the correct plot. Beware possible misconceptions and muddles.

The phone rings and Frank is heard talking to his girlfriend/wife/daughter. He is explaining that he will be late because he has to meet his ex-wife/boss/new student. We learn that he has taken on the extra work to pay for his holiday/drink/ex-wife's maintenance. When his ex-wife/boss/student arrives, we find out her name is Susan/Rhea/Julia, although she calls herself Rita after her mother/Rita Mae West/Rita Hayworth. Rita picks up a copy of *A Passage to India*/*Peer Gynt*/*Howards End* and asks Frank what it is like. Frank says that she can borrow it/she must put it back/she must write an essay on it. We learn from Frank that Rita is a housewife/a hairdresser/a dentist. Frank thinks Rita is very annoying/too stupid to learn/marvellous. He tells her that he is a bad teacher and refuses to teach her/gives her his phone number/leaves the room. Rita agrees/takes no notice/hits him.

Rita returns for her next tutorial and notices that Frank hasn't been drinking/is bruised/is wearing smart clothes. Rita tells Frank that she wants to learn because she wants to go to impress her husband/to be a teacher/to change her life. She has read *Howards End* and thinks it is very inspiring/crap/thought provoking. Rita asks Frank about himself and we discover he is happily married/has split up from his wife/is a homosexual. At the next tutorial, Frank is not happy with Rita's essay/says that Rita is a genius/tells Rita to forget the course. At the following meeting, Frank talks about her essay on *Rubyfruit Jungle*/*Charlie's Angels*/*Peer Gynt*. Rita has written about the wrong book/spelt everything wrong/written only one line. She tells Frank that the ideas in the play made her think about how happy she is/her wedding day/the lives of the people around her. Frank makes her apologise/do the essay again/laugh about it.

**Who? What? Why? When? Where? How?**

1 Who 'phones Frank at the beginning of the play?
2 Where does all the action of this play take place?
3 Why has Frank taken on an Open University student?
4 Why does Rita have trouble opening the door?
5 Why has Rita joined the course?
6 Why does Rita dislike E. M. Forster?
7 What reason does Frank give for his wife leaving him?
8 Why is Rita's essay on Forster not successful?
9 What phrase from Forster does Rita have trouble understanding?
10 How does Frank explain it to her?

**Open quotes**

Identify the scene and the situation; complete the phrase; identify the speaker.

1 'It's that stupid bleedin'...'
2 'There's no suppose about it....'
3 'I don't often consider it actually. I...'
4 'Soon as I walked in here, I said to meself 'Y' can tell...'
5 'It's a mess. But...'
6 'An' it's really temptin'...'
7 'And so, to give me something new to write...'
8 'What I'd actually like to do...'
9 'Possessing a hungry mind... '
10 'You go out and buy yourself a new dress and I'll...'
11 'That's justice for y'. I get failed just cos I'm...'
12 'You mean, it's all right to go...'
13 'You see, a clever answer is not...'
14 'But I don't see any, y' know, culture. I just see...'
15 'He hates me comin' here. It's like...'
16 'If they had the radio...'
17 'I could have told you; but...'
18 'Y' know Peer Gynt? He was...'
19 'Right. That's it. I'll never...'
20 'I'm dead... '

---

## Act 1 Scene 5

*Rita arrives to tell Frank that she has not completed her essay because her husband burnt it, along with the books Frank had lent her. He had found out that she was secretly taking the pill instead of trying to get pregnant. Frank is concerned that Rita's involvement with the course is destroying her marriage, but Rita insists she continues. She says she would rather talk about Chekhov than Denny, but, typically, side-tracks onto Frank's own life. She asks him to tell her about the poetry he used to write and why he gave up. His reply is puzzling: he says he attempted to write literature instead of poetry.*

*After a discussion about the Chekhov and comedy, Rita hits on the idea of going to the theatre: she has never been before. She persuades the reluctant Frank and they go off to see an amateur production of The Importance of Being Earnest.*

### 'I told him I'd only have a baby when I had a choice.'

Rita

Freedom and choice

By now it has become clear that Rita's study is putting a huge strain on her marriage. Denny thinks that the natural way forward for them both is to start a family. He is happy with his lifestyle and does not feel restricted. Rita wants something more than just a natural progression of her relationship. She wants to be able to make an active decision about what to do with her life. How many options does Rita have at present do you think? Do you agree with Denny that the time to make her choices has passed?

### 'You see, the great thing about the booze is that it makes one believe that under all the talk one is actually saying something.'

Frank

Can you make any connections between Frank's inability to face up to life and the way in which Rita describes Denny and others like him? Rita criticises the people in her own class and community for not being able to face up to the dullness of their own lives. Frank, in a way, is exactly the same. He can acknowledge that he is not as happy as he should be, but will not confront this fact or do anything about it. For Frank, drink is an easy way out, just as Valium or 'keg beer' is for those whom Rita describes. In Rita's life it is easier to 'go out and buy another dress'; in Frank's life it is easier to have another drink.

### 'Me? Go to the theatre? God no, I hate the theatre.'

Freedom and choice

Here we see an illustration of Rita's idea of 'choice'. Rita has come from a background that is, in terms of arts, culturally bereft. She has never been to the theatre and, without Frank's encouragement would probably never think to go. She has never, therefore, been given the option of rejecting it, as Frank evidently has done. It is possible, as she tells us at the end of the play, that she may choose to reject the cultural lifestyle that she is about to enter, but at least she will have been able to make that decision on an informed basis. In contrast to Rita, Frank clearly takes for granted all the art and culture he has been given access to. His distaste for the idea of an amateur production highlights this idea.

## Act 1 Scene 6

*Rita bursts into Frank's office, unexpectedly. She is very excited because she has just come back from seeing a professional productions of Macbeth. She needs to tell someone about it, and Frank is the only person who will understand. Frank takes the opportunity to explain the nature of 'tragedy' to Rita. He also invites her to a dinner party at his house. Rita seems rather taken aback, but agrees to go.*

### 'I had to come an' tell y' Frank, last night, I went to the theatre! A proper one, a professional theatre.'

This episode shows that Rita has made great strides forward in her education.

Rita

She has learnt to value and appreciate 'literature' of a very different sort from that which she enjoyed when she first began the course. She is becoming enthused and passionate about the literature she has read and seen, rather than confused and frustrated. Notice, at this moment, how sincere her praise is, and how it comes from herself, rather than anyone else's opinion or ideas.

The examiner will be looking to see that you can identify development in character throughout the play. How has Rita changed? How would you, as a director, depict this change? Think about costume, voice and action. Think, also, about the relationship between Frank and Rita. Are there any ways in which this is beginning to evolve? If so, how?

### 'Look, now, even without ever having heard the story of Macbeth you wanted to shout out, to warn him and prevent him from going on, didn't you?'

*Educating Rita* was obviously not written as a tragedy. It is a funny play which

Character development

provides a great deal of thought provoking comment on many issues. But can you see any connections between Frank's explanation of dramatic tragedy and the characters of Rita and Frank themselves? Is there anything 'inevitable' or unstoppable about Rita's heady quest for an education? Where, like Macbeth, has Rita been 'warned' about what she is getting herself into? And what about Frank? He is an alcoholic who is clearly neglecting his relationship with Julia and who may be forming an emotional and intellectual attachment to his student. Is there anything inevitable about his situation? What can Rita see about him, that he cannot see about himself? It seems that each is powerless to do anything about the other's fate.

### 'I want you to come over to the house.'

Rita is puzzled over Frank's motivation for this. Frank gives as his explanation, 'Because you might enjoy it.' Do you think he is wise in issuing this invitation to Rita and her husband? Do you think he is honest about his reasons?

## Act 1 Scene 7

*Another tutorial. It becomes clear that Rita did not turn up for Frank's dinner party and did not give any proper reason or apology. She explains that she did attempt to go, even though it had caused a big row with her husband, who refused to accompany her. She lost courage, however, when she saw Frank's house and its occupants through the window. She felt overawed and convinced she would say or do the wrong thing. She felt upset that she didn't know which wine to take with her. She also accuses Frank of inviting her so that she can play the role of 'court jester' and amuse his more 'civilised' friends.*

*Frank is angry at the accusation and tells Rita that he invited her simply because he wished to have her company and that if she can't accept that then she should leave and not come back. Rita responds by saying that she has come too far to turn back now. After she left his house, she joined her family down the pub. For a moment she had decided to stop trying to change herself and stay with the world she came from. Then her mother's unhappiness makes her realise that she has to carry on and try to find a different way to live.*

### 'Rita enters, goes straight to her desk and slings her bag on the back of her chair.'

Character development

This is the first time we have seen Rita enter Frank's room and immediately get ready for work. This unusual entrance prepares us for a change of mood and direction. We know immediately that something serious has happened, even though the following conversation is likely to make the audience laugh. Rita's entrance here is symbolic of her new determination to change her life.

### 'I didn't want to come to your house just to play the court jester.'

Rita shows her anger with her natural personality. We see more than ever here how much she hates the very things that Frank admires most about her. She believes that Frank invited her as a freak show who could entertain his other guests, but who could never be taken seriously. What Frank sees as a fresh and natural manner, Rita sees as just stupidity and ignorance. Who do you agree with? Do you think Rita should be ashamed of the way she is?

Rita

### 'I said, "Why are you cryin' mother?" She said, "Because – because we could sing better songs than those".'

This is a crucial moment in the play's dramatic development, and in Rita's development as a character. Her moment of weakness – when she felt she should pack her course in and go back to her old life – was short lived. Her mother's unhappiness at always having to sing the same old songs down the pub represents for Rita her lack of choice and opportunity: her mother wants something different, but does not know what is on offer. Her mother's misery and entrapment steadies Rita's resolve to give herself the freedom that her family hasn't had.

Freedom and choice

## Act 1 Scene 8

*Rita arrives at her tutorial carrying a suitcase. Rita's husband had given her an ultimatum, and she has chosen to leave. She is going to stay with her mother until she finds a place to live. Despite her personal difficulties, she is determined to have a proper tutorial and demands to know what Frank thought about her* Macbeth *essay. Frank reluctantly tells her that it would not be valued by an examiner, although he values it for its honesty and passion. Rita pleads with him to teach her how to write to pass exams, and he admits that he is unwilling to do so because he does not want to change her.*

### 'It's an unashamedly emotional statement about a certain experience.'

We have seen how Rita responds to the literature she has seen and read on a warm, impulsive, emotional level. She felt offended by Forster for not being 'concerned with the poor'; she related *Peer Gynt* to her own life and the lives of those around her; she was excited by *Macbeth* as a powerful story of fate. Frank values these reactions and feels that they are the best part of Rita. She is asking him to teach her to be analytical and critical, and he feels that in doing so he will be robbing her of her own personality.

Rita

Examine Frank's relationship with Rita. What will happen if Rita learns to be analytical and critical, and to think things through before responding to them? Do you think he is right to be unwilling to train Rita in the way she wants? Think about the balance of power in the relationship and how this may be affected by an 'educated' Rita. Think also about your own reaction to the fresh, funny and honest Rita that Russell has presented us with. Would you want her to change? You will have to make your own mind up about the motivation for Frank's reluctance, but it is worth keeping in mind both Frank's attitude towards the changing Rita and Rita's reasons for

Frank

changing herself. Now might be a good time to go back and review scenes one and two in the light of what you have recently discovered.

## Self-test Questions Act 1 Scenes 5–8

**Uncover the plot**

Delete two of the three alternatives given to find the correct plot. Beware misconceptions and muddles.

Rita is upset because her boyfriend/husband/brother has thrown out/stolen/burnt all her books and her essay. She tells Frank that she must pack in the course/carry on with the course/keep it a secret from her husband. Frank tries to persuade her to forget the tutorial and go home/go down the pub with him/go to the doctor. Rita decides that she wants to go clubbing/get a divorce/go to the theatre. Frank is worried that Julia will be jealous/will want to go too/will forbid it. Frank is taken aback when he realises that Rita wants to see an expensive show/a play in a another town/an amateur production.

Rita rushes to see Frank in her lunch hour because she is so excited about her new book/her new lover/the play she has been to see. She has been to see *Hamlet*/*King Lear*/*Macbeth*. As she is about to go back to work, Frank invites her out to dinner/ to see another play/over to his house for dinner.

At the next tutorial, we discover that Rita made a fool of herself at the dinner party/did not turn up to the dinner party/left the party early. She let Frank know by posting her essay with a message through his letter box/ringing beforehand/ throwing a stone through the window. She explained to Frank that she doesn't like Julia/she is a vegetarian/she felt she wouldn't fit in. Afterwards she returned to her family in the pub/at home/in the restaurant. Her mother was drunk and started being aggressive/crying for no real reason/hitting her.

At the next tutorial, Rita turns up with a present/a bottle of whiskey/a suitcase. Denny has discovered that she is ill/still on the pill/that she is having an affair. He told her to forget about the course and stop taking the pill/go to the doctor/give up her lover or to leave. She is staying with Trish/her mother/Frank. Frank tells her that her *Macbeth* essay is the work of a genius/moving, but no good for an exam/too short. She is determined to improve/to get revenge on Denny/to prove Frank wrong.

**Who? What? Why? When? Where? How?**

1 What has happened to Rita's essay and books?
2 What has Denny discovered?
3 Who has Rita heard being described as 'a comic genius?'
4 Why does Frank say he gave up writing poetry?
5 Why does Rita rush to see Frank in her lunch hour?
6 Why does Frank say he invited Rita to his house?
7 What did Rita's mother say she was crying about in the pub?
8 Why has Rita left her husband?
9 Why is Frank reluctant to teach Rita to pass exams?
10 What does Rita do to her *Macbeth* essay?

**Open quotes**

Identify the scene and the situation; complete the phrase; identify the speaker.

1 'Denny found out I was...'
2 'You'd think I was having...'
3 'I've tried to explain to him how you give me room to breathe. Y' just...'
4 'I said to him, y' soft get, even...'
5 'I see him looking at me sometimes...'
6 'He thinks we've got choice because...'
7 'He can burn me books and papers but...'
8 'They didn't tell me to stop drinking, they...'
9 'Poets shouldn't believe...'
10 'If she knew I was at the theatre with an irresistible...'
11 'Life's but a walking shadow...'
12 'Macbeth is flawed by...'
13 'It's fun...'
14 'I can't remember if it's Wilde who's witty and...'
15 'What's funny? I...'
16 'Some stupid woman who gives us all a laugh because...'
17 'She said, 'Because -'
18 'It's an unashamedly...'
19 '... to pass examinations you're going to have to...'
20 If I do something that's crap...'

---

# Act 2 Scene 1

*Rita returns after having been away at summer school. It is clear that some time has elapsed since we last saw her. She tells Frank how exciting it was to be studying in London and how she enjoyed the course. We also discover that she has made several changes in her life, including the acquisition of a new flatmate, Trish. Frank tells Rita about his time in France: Julia left him, but they are now reconciled. Rita is now impatient with Frank's stuffy office, and wants to go outside, or open the window. Frank is reluctant. Rita is also disappointed that Frank is still drinking heavily.*

*Frank has planned to teach Rita Blake's poetry this term. He is somewhat taken aback that Rita has already covered this in her summer school.*

## 'And what is this vision, returning from the city?'

Notice how we are given the details of Rita's absence implicitly and indirectly: it is delivered to us through dialogue, in the same way as other information in the play. There are other clues, however, which indicate a jump in time. We are not introduced to the idea of summer school at the end of Act 1, so we can assume that several tutorials have taken place between Rita's split from her husband and her departure for summer school. She talks of her late night conversations with her new friends, and her trips to the theatres. Significantly, Rita enters wearing new clothes (although second hand ones). How does this compare to the Rita of a few

**Character development**

scenes back, who was breathless with excitement because she had just seen her first ever theatre production? Does this change seem sudden and unnatural, or has the author managed to make it seem like a natural process of character development?

Presentation of character development is an important aspect of the staging of a play. See the specimen coursework question on page 55 for a discussion of how you might show Rita to be changing and developing.

### '... so I did it, I asked him the question.' *Rita*
### 'Trish?' *Frank*

It is not just the characters which are developed in this scene, but their role in relation to one another. We have been used to Rita being completely dependent upon Frank for her intellectual development, and to her sharing the problems of her personal life with him. Now, however, she has another source of intellectual stimulation, and some other friends with whom she can share her thoughts. Frank has guided Rita through the beginning of her course and prepared her for studying alone, but it is summer school that gives Rita the confidence she has been lacking. We feel that she is on her way to being able to talk 'seriously, confidently, with knowledge', because she is no longer afraid of being laughed at.

Personal relationships

In contrast, Frank is quiet. Whilst Rita has given up smoking, Frank has returned to drinking heavily. Frank is unaware of important changes that have taken place in Rita's life: we, the audience, are used to Rita sharing all her personal circumstances with Frank. She is beginning to need him less, and to take on the role of mentor rather than pupil. She gently chides him for continuing to drink, and tries to persuade him to continue to write, by giving him an engraved pen. She is starting to ask questions, not only about literature, but about the wisdom of her tutor. Turn back to the earlier scenes now and compare Frank and Rita's interaction to that of their first meeting: how has it changed?

Character development

Summer school has obviously had a big impact on Rita. For a discussion of the effect of summer school on Rita's development, and the inevitability or otherwise of what follows, see question 2 of the example exam questions on page 51.

### 'I'm not surprised, my dear. It hasn't been opened for generations.'

The window in Frank's study represents Rita's 'view' of what she thinks she wants to achieve: remember how she wistfully talked of the students sitting outside on the grass. It is symbolic, then, that she wishes to have her tutorial outside, or at least to open the window. The room which she once described as 'perfect' now seems stuffy and confining. On a literal level, this is because the weather has grown hotter, but it is also symbolic of Rita's growth. Where the room once offered freedom and escape, it is now presented as being almost suffocating. Why is it no surprise that Frank refuses to hold his tutorial outside or that his window is jammed shut? Think back, also, to the sticking door at the beginning of the play. How does this fit with the way we view Frank and his study.

Character development

Frank

### 'Of course; you don't do Blake without doing innocence and experience, do y'?'

There are many examples of Rita's growing independence from Frank in this scene, but this last one clearly shows her transition from an admiring pupil to a rather cocky student. Frank has saved up his favourite poet for Rita, sure that she will understand in a way his other students do not. There is something rather poignant about her rejection of his offering. He presents the poet to Rita as if it were a prize or gift, and seems crushed by her response: again we are left feeling that he is rather redundant. Significantly, the poems are Blake's *Songs of Innocence and Experience*. Rita, too, has embarked on a journey from innocence to experience.

Rita

## Act 2 Scene 2

*Rita arrives for her tutorial. She has adopted a rather affected accent, because her flatmate, Trish, has said that she needs to cultivate a beautiful voice. Frank is horrified, and Rita soon drops the act. She begins to tell Frank about her conversation with the students on the grass beneath Frank's window. She is clearly less overawed by them than she used to be, and seems pleased and flattered by their attention. Frank is clearly uneasy about her new confidence and her association with the students. Rita asks him about her essay and he replies that it is good as the work of his other students.*

### 'As Trish says there is not a lot of point in discussing beautiful literature in an ugly voice.'

Rita drops her silly voice and reverts to normal, implying that she is just joking.

How far do you think that this is true? How much of an influence does 'Trish' have on her, and what sort of a person is she? Look back to the last scene: Rita describes her as 'unpretentious'. How true do you think this might be?

Personal relationships

'For students they don't half come out with some rubbish y' know.'

Compare this statement to Rita's awe and envy of students in the first few scenes. There is still some envy implied in her comment that 'They can just jump into a bleedin' van…' but this feeling is based on envy of their personal freedom, not their intellectual abilities. She has begun to achieve some of what she set out to do: she is talking confidently with people from whom she used to shy away; she is writing essays suitable for exams. You will recall that Rita's main objective was to 'discover herself.' Do you feel she has achieved this yet? Rita has certainly gained knowledge, but the question is – how wisely will she use it?

Freedom and choice

### 'Well – you've got your results to wait for…"

There seems to be something rather desperate about Frank's feeble reason for Rita not to go away with the other students. Why is Frank so worried about Rita's integration with the other students? Do you think he has become so dependent on Rita that he is fearful of losing her? Or of losing influence over her? Is he displaying the natural concern of a guide or mentor? It is tempting to read a sexual or romantic motive into his speech and actions: it seems that Russell leads us part of the way towards this idea so that we half expect a sexual or romantic issue to appear. Whichever interpretation you settle for, it is clear that Frank is resisting Rita's new independence.

Frank

## Act 2 Scene 3

*Rita is already settled in Frank's study when he enters, very drunk, complaining that the students have reported him for being too drunk to lecture properly. He tells Rita that he is unlikely to be sacked, but might be sent away on sabbatical. Rita is less sympathetic than he expects. She argues than his behaviour is unfair on his students, and then suggests they hold the tutorial another time. Frank does not want her to go and tries to pull himself together to hold the lesson. He is disappointed with Rita's latest essay on Blake because she has not agreed with his particular interpretation, but has turned to others for their opinions. They begin to argue: Rita defends her right to have her own opinions; Frank claims that her opinions are simply drawn from others. Rita ends by telling Frank that she needs less help from him now.*

## 'Completely off my cake. I know.'

In this scene we see how much Rita has affected Frank. He refers to a phrase coined by Rita much earlier in their relationship and then goes on to say that he told his students about her interpretation of 'assonance': 'getting the rhyme wrong'. He is clearly trying to hang on to the fresh and uneducated 'old' Rita. It is significant that the further away Rita moves from him, the more he drinks.

Frank

## 'Well it's hardly fair on them if their lecturer's so pissed that he's falling off the rostrum.'

Character development

How do you think Rita's response differs from that of the first couple of scenes? Remember her awed and admiring comment in Scene 1: she claims to like him 'Because you're a crazy, mad piss artist who wants to throw his students through the window.' Do you think that this is a change for the better? Or, like Frank, do you feel that she has been ruined?

## 'I sincerely hope so, my dear.'

Character development

Some of the irony of Frank's situation is spelt out for us here, and it is made even more clear in the subsequent scenes. Frank has, almost against his own will, taught Rita to lose her own emotional and subjective responses to what she has read. He has taught her to be objective and critical and to learn independently. As a result, she has also learnt to be objective and critical about him and his ideas. What he feared has taken place: she has lost a part of herself forever. Rita's viewpoint is different, of course. She feels that she has gained something and has learnt to think independently. Who do you agree with? Has Frank made a monster, as he later suggests?

Rita

Your examiner will be looking for evidence of your ability to see how characters develop and change. We have already dealt with some aspects of this, but it is worth looking at the *language* development now. Just as Frank has started to adopt some of Rita's old phrases, Rita has started to use a much wider vocabulary and less colloquial speech. The result is a more authoritative style of speech. She is still hesitant at times, but she is able to challenge Frank in an articulate and credible manner.

One additional point: have you noticed how Frank is insistent on addressing Rita as 'my dear', especially when she seems to want to challenge him? Why do you think he does this? This issue of 'the language of power' might be worth incorporating into an essay on character development and language.

## Act 2 Scene 4

*Rita arrives late for her tutorial. She apologises, saying that she was 'talking' and she didn't notice the time. She offers to leave and promises to be on time next week. Frank tells her to stay because he is disconcerted that she has not told him that she has left the hairdresser's shop. Rita does not think that this is an important point, but Frank seems upset that she no longer shares things with him. Frank suggests that she no longer wants to come to his tutorials, but Rita denies this. We discover that she had cancelled her last meeting with him.*

*Throughout the conversation, Frank has been drinking. Rita angrily tells him that if he were to stop drinking he would be able to talk about what 'matters' and it might be worth her while to attend his tutorials. In response, Frank questions her ability to recognise what does or doesn't matter. He then takes his own poetry out of his desk and asks her to critically assess it.*

### 'It struck me that there was a time when you used to tell me everything.'

We see here an even stronger indication of Frank's emotional involvement with his student. It is natural and inevitable that, as she learns more, Rita will become less reliant on Frank's input and support. It is Frank's job to give Rita the tuition she requires, and yet he seems to need or want something in return. The balance of power in their relationship has shifted from one extreme to the other, and it is Frank who is the more needy character now. The irony, of course, lies in the way that the change has been facilitated by Frank himself.

**Personal relationships**

### 'We talk about what's important, Frank, and we leave out the boring details for those who want them.'

Remember Rita's complaint at the beginning of the play – that the people around her do not discuss things 'that matter.' What does she mean by this? What are the things that matter to Rita now? For Frank, the kind of 'boring, irrelevant detail' that Rita no longer wishes to discuss, was valuable and represented real life. Earlier on, when Rita's enthusiasm for study was putting a strain on her marriage, Frank advised her to put her relationship first: 'When art and literature begin to take the place of life itself, perhaps it's time to…'. Do you think that was sound advice? Do you think that Rita has lost touch with what life is about? Or do you applaud her for raising herself above her mundane existence?

**Rita**

**Character development**

**'Is Mr Tyson one of your customers?'**
**'You really don't have to put in the odd appearance out of sentimentality... I'd rather you spared me that.'**

Personal relationships

How far does Frank's involvement with Rita stretch? Do you think he feels like a parent who is watching his little girl grow up and need him less? Do you think he is simply a good friend who is watching helplessly as Rita walks further and further away from her real self? Or do you think he has fallen in love with her, and is jealous of her fascination with the students around her? It might be worth bearing in mind that Frank does have a stable relationship of his own and that, away from the study which has become so familiar to us, he has his own, entirely separate life. How do we account then, for his intense interest and attachment to Rita? Perhaps it is because she is, in a sense, his 'product.' Does he feel responsible for Rita's new life?

Frank

**'A critical assessment of a lesser known English poet. Me.'**

The scene closes with Frank challenging Rita to assess his own work. Why does he ask her to do this at this point? Now might be a good moment to look back over Frank's previous references to his work. Frank gave up writing because he was trying too hard to make good 'literature.' What does he think of his work now?

# Self-test Questions Act 2 Scenes 1–4

**Uncover the plot**

Delete two of the three alternatives given to find the correct plot. Beware possible misconceptions and muddles.

Rita has arrived back from having a baby/summer school in London/hospital. Frank tells her that during his trip to France/Spain/Australia Julia left him. Rita tells Frank that she has a new pet/husband/flatmate. It is hot weather and Rita is not content to stay in the study/read books/listen to Frank. She is disappointed that he is still smoking/writing/drinking. Frank wants to introduce Rita to a poet called Yeats/Blake/Byron. He is taken aback when he discovers that she has already covered him with Trish/at summer school/at school. Rita becomes more friendly with the bursar/hairdressers/other students. She seems to have a special interest in one called Tiger/Panther/Monkey. She is pleased when Frank tells her that her last essay is going to be published/is as good as the other students'/made him laugh.

Frank is very drunk/happy/angry when Rita arrives for her next tutorial. Rita suggests that they forget the tutorial/go to a party/have counselling. Frank is unhappy with her latest essay because it is too short/it is rubbish/it is not her own opinion. When Rita is late for her next tutorial, Frank 'phones her house/reports her/'phones the shop. He discovers that she has changed her job and is working in a bistro/an office/a pub. Frank and Rita argue and Frank presents her with a detention/his diary/his poetry. He asks her to burn it/hide it/write an assessment of it.

**Who? What? Why? When? Where? How?**

1 Where has Rita been just before the act starts?
2 What change has Rita made in her life since she last saw Frank?
3 What has Rita brought back from London for Frank?
4 What is strange about Rita when she arrives for her tutorial in Scene 2?
5 Who does Frank think that Rita is going to fall in love with?
6 Why do the students complain about Frank?
7 Why does Frank dislike Rita's Blake essay?
8 What book does Frank say he has read, that Rita once told him about?
9 Why is Frank upset that Rita has changed her job?
10 What does Frank ask Rita to do at the end of Scene 4?

**Open quotes**

Identify the scene and the situation; complete the phrase; identify the speaker.

1 'What are you talking about? London or...'
2 'It was right on the tip of my tongue to say...'
3 'Honest to God, I stood up, an'...'
4 'Anyway, the holiday's over, you're back, even...'
5 ' Well any analogy will...'
6 'You will understand Blake; they over complicate him, Rita, but...'
7 'As Trish says, there is not a lot of point in discussing...'
8 'For students, they don't half come out with...'
9 'It's all right for them. They can just jump into...'
10 'To get the sack it'd have to be rape on a grand scale; and...'
11 'Or maybe they did it because they're a crowd of mealy-mouthed pricks...'
12 'I mean if that poem's only about the blossom then...'
13 'It struck me that there was a time when...'
14 'You really don't have to put in the odd appearance out of...'
15 'No sentimentality, no subjectivity. Just pure criticism. A critical...'

---

## Act 2 Scene 5

*Rita turns up at Frank's study unexpectedly. She has stayed up all night reading Frank's poetry with her flatmate, Trish. She is almost breathless with enthusiasm for his work. In her attempt to convey her feelings she quotes Trish's opinion. Instead of being pleased with her opinion, Frank is angry that she does not see things as she did when she started the course. He acknowledges the part he has played in this unwelcome transition by comparing himself to the creator of Frankenstein. Rita is also angry and accuses him of resenting her newly found education, and tells him that he takes his own privileges for granted. The scene ends with Frank discovering that Rita dropped her adopted name ages ago: he is the only person to still address her in that way. Rita leaves the room while Frank is calling out alternative 'literary' names for her to adopt.*

### 'At first we just saw it as contemporary poetry in its own right...'

Rita is gushing in her approval of Frank's poetry. She has sat up all night reading it and seems to be sincere. Her ability to appreciate Frank's 'literature' seems to put the seal on her education. How do you expect Frank to respond to her enthusiasm? Notice here how she quotes Trish, her flatmate, as well as giving her own opinions. This reliance on other people's thoughts is certain to annoy Frank, given their conversation in Scene 3. Rita is proud of her ability to recognise good 'literature', and to her this appraisal of Frank's poetry is like finally arriving at her destination. To Frank, however, it is the final confirmation of what he has been dreading.

Rita

### 'She wrote a little Gothic number called *Frankenstein*.'

Frank plays on Rita's pride in being able to recognise literary allusions (references to other works, often rather obscure) by using an allusion to summarise their relationship. He alludes to *Frankenstein*, implying that he, like Dr Frankenstein, has created a monster which is now out of control. As has been suggested in previous scenes, he has been partly responsible for Rita's change and new life, but he now hates what he has done.

Literature

### 'I've got a room full of books. I know what clothes to wear, what wine to buy, what plays to see, what papers and books to read.' *Rita*

### 'Have you come all this way for so very, very little?' *Frank*

With whom do you have more sympathy? It is one of Russell's strengths that he builds his characters so carefully that we can understand both of them and they both provoke our compassion. You may find, though, that you can sympathise with one more than the other. Do you share Frank's frustration and sadness at watching Rita lose her honesty and naiveté? Do you feel that Rita is wrong to judge everything by its worth in terms of 'high culture'? Or do you sympathise with Rita's view that Frank resents her being his equal, and that he is so spoilt and cynical that he doesn't appreciate his education? Perhaps both of them, in their own ways, need to review their outlook on life and learning.

Personal relationships

### 'Rita? Nobody calls me Rita but you. I dropped that pretentious crap as soon as I saw it for what it was.'

This final conversation, centring on Rita's name, is heavily symbolic of Rita's change and her break from Frank. 'Rita' was the name belonging to the old way of life, a name that Frank has been clinging on to, hoping to resurrect something

Character development

from the past. That Frank did not know that Rita now uses her proper name emphasises how far removed they now are from those times. In a sense, he doesn't even know who she is any more.

## Act 2 Scene 6

*Frank tries to phone Rita to let her know when her exam is. He leaves a message with her flatmate, Trish.*

### 'Yes... well could you tell her that I have – erm – I've entered her for her examination.'

Personal relationships

This is a very short scene which establishes the gulf between Frank and Rita: they clearly have not been in touch for a while. We also feel that Frank's bumbling attempt to let Rita know about her exam may be his way of trying to make peace. By doing this he is making a concession to her new life. The exam itself represents the end of Rita's course and the culmination of her 'education'. We see in the next scene that she has learnt much more than simply understanding what she has read. The exam tests her wisdom and her ability to choose.

## Act 2 Scene 7

*It is Christmas-time. Rita returns to Frank's study to find him arriving with tea chests, ready to pack up his belongings. He has been given a two year sabbatical to Australia for his drunken behaviour. Rita tells him that she has returned to thank him for being a good teacher. She sat her exam, and answered it well, but only after thinking through some of the things he had said to her. Her flatmate's attempted suicide has made her realise that there was some truth in his accusations.*

*Frank asks if Rita would like to accompany him to Australia, but Rita avoids answering and tells him that she has several other plans to think about. Frank presents her with a dress as a parting gift. Rita announces that there is only one thing she can give him in return for all he has done: she sits him down, finds a pair of scissors and begins to cut his hair.*

### 'It's like Trish, y' know me flatmate, I thought she was so cool and together – I came home the other night an' she'd tried to top herself.'

It is not until Rita's final exam that she realises the true worth of her education, and learns to value it for the right reasons. Trish already had everything that Rita so desperately wanted, and yet she can be no happier than those people Rita described from her own community. All the high culture, literature and clever conversation that were a part of her life clearly had not given

Class, culture and education

her freedom. Perhaps Frank is right and these are not the things that 'matter'. They may be good things in themselves, but an education can provide more than simply a cultured lifestyle. Do you agree?

**'But I chose not to. I had a choice. I did the exam.'**
**'I might go to France. I might go to me mother's. I might even have a baby. I dunno. I'll make a decision, I'll choose.'**

Here Rita spells out exactly what she has gained, aside from the trappings of an intellectual social scene. She has gained control over her life: she has chosen to write her exam well; she will choose what she will do next. Instead of simply being propelled down a route decided for her by others, as she has described to Frank in previous scenes, she now has the power to make decisions about her life.

Freedom and choice

The first two of Rita's 'choices' sound rather trivial, but in articulating her short-term choices she is reminding us of the many possibilities that are open to her now in the wider sense. Even if she doesn't 'use' her new qualification in a direct way, she at least has the power to decide this. The last of Rita's choices 'I might even have a baby' is significant because she is contemplating the very thing that she was trying to avoid when she started the course. Do you think that this is just leading her back to square one? Or is it different now? If you think it is, then why? This is a key point in the play.

**'I hear very good things about Australia. Things are just beginning there.'**

It is not only Rita who is embarking on a new phase of her life: Frank, too, is about to make a new start. He has been consistently characterised as stale, lacking in idealism and trapped in a situation of his own making. A country where 'things are just beginning' seems an appropriate place for Frank to go, even if he has not made a choice. Frank has been presented as someone with no real control over his life: he is dominated by his drink habit, his girlfriend, his college authorities, even his own apathy. The fresh start in Australia signifies some hope for his future.

Frank

**'It's – erm – well, it's er – it's a dress really. I bought it some time ago – for erm – for an educated woman friend – of mine.'**

Frank's presentation of a dress for Rita reminds us of Rita's statement in Act 1: 'I haven't had a new dress in twelve months. An' I'm not gonna get one either, not till – till I pass my first exam.' It is Frank's acknowledgement of how much she has achieved, and of her right to enjoy at least some of the material trappings that she longed for before the completion of her course.

Class, culture and education

**'I never thought there was anythin' I could give you. But there is. Come here, Frank.'**

The play ends, as Russell himself puts it, on 'a joke, a gag.' Rita's words lead us further in the direction of suspecting some sexual involvement between the two. Our expectations prove wrong, however, as she finds a pair of scissors and starts to give him a haircut.

Why do you think Russell chose to end the play with a comic moment? What effect does it have? What effect would ending the play in a serious way have had? Can you think of an appropriate alternative ending? A good exercise might be to try and write your own ending to the play and to comment upon your desired effect.

It is very important to keep in mind the 'performance' aspect of any play you study. Whilst Russell's play is engrossing and thought provoking as 'literature', it was conceived to be performed on a stage in front of an audience. Many exam or coursework questions will reflect this aspect of the text. It would be worth acting out certain scenes to prepare for your response to a question like this. Try different ways of acting out the same scene, and give careful consideration to costume, setting and how the characters change in their physical appearance.

One of the National Curriculum requirements for English is to show that you can comment on how a text has been adapted for different mediums. *Educating Rita* is a successful film as well as a stage play. Watch the film carefully and note the changes made by the filmmaker. Why have these changes been made? Were they necessary? Which held most appeal for you? Why? You could base a coursework assignment on these observations.

# Self-test Questions Act 2 Scenes 5–7

**Uncover the plot**

Delete two of the three alternatives given to find the correct plot. Beware possible misconceptions and muddles.

Rita arrives at Frank's study unexpectedly because she wants to tell Frank that he is a bad writer/she has lost his work/he is a brilliant poet. Frank compares what he has done to Rita to a novel called *Frankenstein/Dracula/Howards End*. Rita scornfully tells him that she no longer uses the name 'Rita'/she no longer likes poetry/he should change his own name.

Despite having quarrelled, Frank still 'phones Rita to apologise/invite her to dinner/tell her when her exam is. When they next meet, Frank is too drunk to talk/packing to go to Australia/about to go on holiday to France. Rita has sat her exam and done well/written a one line answer/walked out of it. She has come to blame Frank for letting her down/to ask Frank to marry her/to thank Frank for being a good teacher. Frank asks Rita to go with him/tells her to get lost/passes out. Rita says that she doesn't know what she will do, but whatever it is, she will ask Frank's advice/choose for herself/have it forced upon her. Frank gives Rita a new dress/a haircut/a kiss. Rita then gives Frank a kiss/a book of poems/a haircut.

**Who? What? Why? When? Where? How?**

1 Why does Rita arrive unexpectedly at Frank's study in Scene 5?
2 Why does Rita arrive unexpectedly at Frank's study in Scene 7?.
3 What does Rita say is 'pretentious crap'?
4 Why does Frank phone Rita in Scene 6?
5 Where has Frank been sent, for being drunk during lectures?
6 What question did Rita have to answer in her exam?
7 What has happened to make Rita question the value of what she has learnt?
8 What does Rita say is the best thing that Frank has given her?
9 What does Frank ask her to do?
10 What does Rita do to Frank at the end of the play?

**Open quotes**

Identify the scene and the situation; complete the phrase; identify the speaker.

1 'If you mean am I still this side of…'
2 'Oh, I've done a fine…'
3 '… from now on I shall insist on being known as Mary,…'
4 'You'll find more wit in the telephone book, and,…'
5 'Found a better song to sing, have you? No – you've found a different song, that's all – and…'
6 'You stupid… nobody…'
7 'It's like Trish, y' know, me flatmate, I thought she was so cool and together – I came home…'
8 'It'd be good for us to leave a place that's just finishing for…'
9 'I'll make a decision…'
10 'I'm gonna take…'

# How to write an examination essay

Most of you will be using *Educating Rita* as a set text for your formal examination. In order to be ready for the examination, you will need to have carefully studied the plot, characters, themes and issues of the text. You will also be expected to have considered the play from a 'performance' angle. Reading this guide in an active manner will have helped you to achieve all of this, but you will also need to learn how to write an examination essay so that you do not lose marks. Study the following guidelines and then read the sample examination questions.

## Answer the question asked

Many candidates lose marks because they have misread or misinterpreted the question, under pressure of time. Make sure that you know what the question requires from you and that you answer it directly. There is no time for waffle or diversion in an exam! Another common mistake happens when students have written a *similar* essay for practice *before* the exam. In trying to rewrite their old essay, they fail to notice that the exam essay is asking something slightly different. It hardly ever pays to learn essays off by heart.

For example, the question, 'Explore the reasons for Rita's need to change' is asking something different from, 'Examine the social and personal implications of the changes Rita makes'. It could be tempting, however, to ignore the subtle differences if you have an essay already prepared for one of the questions.

## Do not just retell the story

The skills required for just retelling the plot are not enough to get you much beyond a 'G' at GCSE. The examiner assumes you know the story and accepts that you may have to relate a little of it to show what you mean. It wins no marks, however, and should be kept to a minimum. In an exam, you will be asked to *explore*, *examine*, *imagine*, *describe* but never to simply *retell*. For example, if you are asked to 'comment on the way in which Rita changes throughout the play' you will need to examine the reasons for Rita's change and the impact it has on her and others. You are not asked to simply say what has happened to her.

## Plan your essay

You should always make time to do a short plan of your answer, however worried about time you are. Make a list of points to be included and then decide on the best order for them. It is often a good idea to check them off as you are writing, to make sure you do not miss any. Doing a plan helps you to avoid one of the most common pitfalls of examinations: failing to answer the question properly. This 'thinking' time is essential for good organisation and structure of your essay.

## Starting to write

The opening few sentences can often be the most difficult to write, and can take the longest to think about. It is essential that they actually *address the question* because this will set your essay off on the right lines from the very beginning. The first few lines should give a clear indication of the kind of response you will give to the question. For example, your opening line to the question asking you to 'comment on the way Rita changes' might be: 'Rita initially changes in response to personal, social and cultural circumstances which she feels are trapping and restricting her'. You can then go on to examine the different ways in which Rita is trapped and the way in which this leads her to be unquestioning in her acceptance of another culture.

## Quotation

You should quote in order to back up the points you are making. There is no point in quoting lengthy chunks of the text; this wins you no marks. Only quote as much as you need to prove your point. Four lines at a time is probably the absolute maximum.

## Technical points to keep in mind

- Write your essay in formal English. Never use slang and do not write as if you were speaking.
- Avoid using contractions. Write '*should have*' not '*should've*'.
- Organise your essay into paragraphs.
- Check your spelling. Accurate spelling is rewarded. Careless spelling mistakes create a bad impression.
- Use punctuation appropriately and correctly. Do not confuse the possessive apostrophe with plurals.
- Take care over the presentation of your essay. Write legibly and avoid crossing out too many words or sentences. Many crossings out indicate a lack of planning.

## Example questions

Below are two examples of the kinds of questions you may expect in your exam. An *outline* of a model answer has been supplied for each question. You will find it useful to write full-length versions of these plans, incorporating references from the text to back up the ideas.

**1** Read the opening of the play to 'D' y' get a lot like me?' (Rita). In what ways is this extract a good introduction to the play's main characters and themes? Do you think that Willy Russell has made his opening dramatic and entertaining? *MEG (specimen) 1998*

- All our information about the characters and ideas in the play must come from dialogue and visual clue, since there are no minor characters to provide us with information, and there is no narrator to guide us through events. Therefore we must look carefully at stage directions and what the characters reveal to each other.
- We are introduced to Frank's alcoholism right from the start. The initial few moments of the play make it clear that this character will be dominated by his need to drink. There is also a subtle connection made between his drunkenness and his academic life: his stash of alcohol is hidden amongst his books. The moment is comic, but clearly defines Frank's character for us.
- The telephone call acts as a device to give us information and set the scene. Our impression of Frank as an alcoholic is confirmed; we learn that he has a girlfriend or wife; we discover that he is waiting to tutor an Open University student; the ongoing motif of Julia's cooking is introduced. We are given a great deal of information about Frank in a very short space of time. It is easy to absorb the information because it is partly visual, and the monologue is comic. The seemingly 'incidental' nature of the information (as part of the humour) means that we can quickly become involved in the plot: there are no distractions.
- Frank's attitude towards Open University students is dismissive. It describes an elitist attitude towards education that Russell goes on to explore through his characters.
- Rita's entrance has maximum impact on the audience, and provides an effective contrast to Frank. We have just listened to a rather bored, cynical monologue from Frank and it stands in opposition to Rita's outburst as she comes into the study. She is direct and forthright, with little subtlety. Her irreverent behaviour seems out of place in the academic's study.

- Rita's attitude that Frank should 'get on with' fixing the door handle is a good introduction to her pro-active attitude to life. Frank's failure to 'get round' to fixing the door sums up his inability to take control of his life.
- The door itself is representative of the staleness of Frank's life. Obviously very few people have a need to use Frank's door: it seems to shut Frank in, and the world out.
- Rita is unable to respond to Frank's polite, formal enquiries about her name. This reflects her informal nature and her distance from Frank's world.
- Rita moves around rather than simply sitting down as you might expect. She notices the things around her. She also flits easily from one subject to another. This prepares us for her restlessness and inability to concentrate, but also for her quickness of mind, and curiosity.
- Rita's observation about Frank's picture foreshadows the way she will make Frank appreciate things that he has grown bored of, or taken for granted. She has original ideas about the work of art, albeit uninformed ones. This incident shows us the innocence and independence that Frank fears she will lose by gaining knowledge.
- Despite Frank's cynical confidence at the beginning of the scene, Rita ends up taking control of the conversation, while Frank is too flustered to proceed with the formalities of their tutorial. This is an indication of how their relationship will continue.
- There is a touch of irony in the last words of the extract 'D' y' get a lot like me?' Rita is referring to Open University students, but it also becomes clear that Frank has never really met anyone like Rita in his life.
- The most important features of each character are presented to us with much humour and they are effectively contrasted with each other. This extract also begins to open up some of the important themes of the play, such as attitudes towards class and education. We are cleverly prepared for what is to follow.
- The stark contrast between the two characters heightens the dramatic impact of this opening. The confused exchange between the two characters is simple, and yet highly amusing. Rita's use of slang and colloquial language is useful in making Frank seem rather stuffy and over-formal, and the difference produces humour – along with Frank's astonishment.
- The visual humour is also very entertaining. Frank's hunt for his alcohol and Rita's struggle with the door are good 'gags' which complement the witty dialogue.

- Russell succeeds in both entertaining and informing, without overloading us. He grabs our attention by using the initial visual joke, and sustains it by the amusing dialogue between the characters.

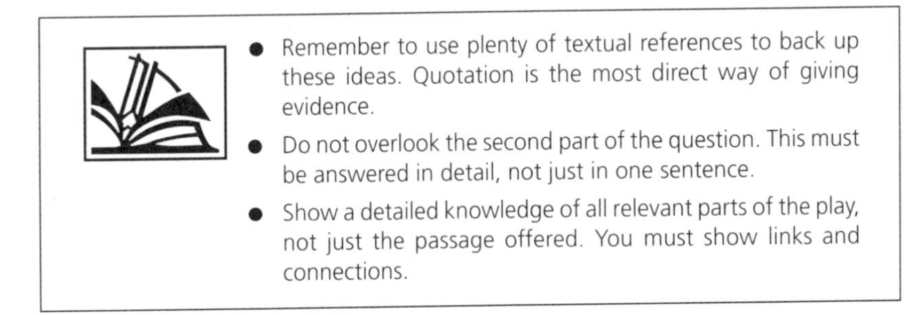

- Remember to use plenty of textual references to back up these ideas. Quotation is the most direct way of giving evidence.
- Do not overlook the second part of the question. This must be answered in detail, not just in one sentence.
- Show a detailed knowledge of all relevant parts of the play, not just the passage offered. You must show links and connections.

**2** Read Act 2, Scene 1 carefully. How does the experience of summer school challenge Rita's view of the world and is what follows inevitable?

*London (Edexcel) specimen 1998*

- Up until this point Rita's pursuit of her education has been a solitary one. Now she has come in contact with others who share the same goals. The experience is a motivating one.
- Until now, Frank has been her sole influence and mentor in the literary world. This means he is able to impress upon her his own values and ideas. Now she has had access to a whole range of other people's ideas and knowledge. This leads her to challenge Frank's views in a way she couldn't have before (for example the Blake poem).
- Rita has not just come into contact with other ways of looking at literature, but with a whole new 'culture'. She has thrown herself into it wholeheartedly.
- It is at this point that Frank's study begins to be presented as stuffy and suffocating. She is ready for new influences and experiences, but Frank does not want to let her go. The jammed window represents the restrictive atmosphere of the study and Rita's need to look beyond the single influence of Frank.
- Rita has begun to realise the wealth of opportunity that is in front of her. Her family had made her feel that twenty-six was too old to be learning and having a good time: she was 'odd' because she had not yet started a family. Meeting other students at summer school has made her see that there is no 'set' time to achieve things in life and that it is acceptable to continue to grow and develop.
- Summer school has also helped her to have confidence in her abilities and to have faith in the validity of her questions. Her tutors are helpful

and enthusiastic and do not condemn her lack of knowledge. It is the first time she has had the opportunity to try out her opinions on anyone except Frank. She is also meeting people who take pleasure in the discussion of literature, perhaps more than Frank.

- Rita's visit to summer school is a turning point in her education. It exposes her to new influences and to others who consider the pursuit of knowledge at any time in life to be a worthwhile and pleasurable activity.
- Her recent adventures can only confirm her fears of Frank's degeneration and staleness. She still holds on to her wish to inspire him to change, but it is obvious that it will become harder for her to do this as she becomes more involved with her new life.
- It would be very hard for Rita to go back to her old life now, even if she wanted to. Her progress from this point is unstoppable. There is still a marked contrast, however, in her own colloquial language and the beauty of the poetry she has been studying. She still has difficulty in reconciling the two worlds.
- Frank describes Rita's breaking away from him as 'inevitable', and in a way he is right. Much later in the play, Rita compares their relationship to one between a child and a parent. The child is sheltered by the parent in the first few years of life, but is gradually introduced to a variety of people and experiences, most of which are a great deal more exciting than the protective parent. It is natural that Rita would be attracted to other, younger and more dynamic influences, and that she will feel the need for more than Frank to mould her views. In this sense it is inevitable.
- There is also an allusion to *Macbeth* and the discussion about tragedy held earlier. We realise later that, although Rita becomes critical of Frank, her first teacher, she fails to become critical of anything in her exciting new life, despite Frank's warnings. Frank tells her that she should not be stuck in his study forever, but at the same time sees Rita's descent into superficiality as inevitable. He realises that he has to let her go, but has become so dependent on her that he sees her independence from him as a betrayal. In another, more 'tragic' sense, this outcome, too, is inevitable. It is inevitable that she will make mistakes, having had so little experience of the 'cultured' world, and it is inevitable that his strange attachment to her will have to be broken.
- Summer school opens up a whole new world of possibilities for Rita. Her sudden plunge into this world, after being so sheltered by having Frank as her only influence, could be said to make what follows inevitable.

This is not the only 'right' answer to this question. It would be good practice to attempt the opposite argument: that there is no inevitability.

Make sure you expand on all the points in your own way, and use plenty of supporting references from the text.

Ensure a detailed exploration of both parts of the question. The second part gives you an opportunity to show your skills of argument.

# How to write a coursework essay

Those of you who are studying *Educating Rita* for a coursework assignment may have been asked to include a comparative element in your essay. This might involve comparing *Educating Rita* with another modern play, or it might ask you to compare the playscript with the director's treatment of it in a production you have seen. It might even ask you to make comparisons within the play, for example, to contrast Frank with Rita. In any of these cases it is important that you make a genuine comparison and you do not deal with each comparative element separately. In the case of two modern plays, it is not sufficient to retell the story of both and then write a few concluding lines to show similarities. Your comparative element should form the bulk of your essay.

If you are comparing *Educating Rita* with another modern play, select the text carefully. There must be some similarity of theme and idea in order to allow comparisons to be made. Look for a text which deals with education or class issues, or is based on a pupil-teacher relationship. Another Russell play might be a good idea – 'Our Day Out' or 'Stags and Hens'.

Make sure your **title** is specific. It should direct you to a particular task, not just give you a vague heading to work from. For example, 'Examine problems of class and culture which arise in *Educating Rita* and *An Inspector Calls*' gives you more guidance than 'Class and Culture in *Educating Rita* and *An Inspector Calls*'.

### How long should my essay be?

Most coursework should be a minumum of 500 words, essentially it should be as long as it needs to be to answer the question fully and well. Check with your teacher for specific word limits. Remember that a long essay is not necessarily a good essay; make sure that everything you say is relevant and concise. Do not repeat yourself. The examiner will be prepared to read a long essay if it is worthwhile, but will lose patience with waffle or irrelevant material.

### Writing the coursework essay

- It is essential that you make a plan before you begin to write. Think about the key points of the play that are relevant to your essay.
- Always do a rough draft of your coursework. Listen to the suggestions that your teacher makes after reading your rough draft and amend your draft accordingly.
- Check your best draft carefully for spelling, punctuation and grammar.

## Quotation

You should quote in order to back up the points you are making. There is no point in quoting lengthy chunks of the text; this wins you no marks. Simply quote as much as you need to prove your point. Four lines at a time is probably the absolute maximum.

## Example question

Below is an example of the kind of question you may expect for your coursework assignment. An *outline* of a model answer has been supplied for the question. You will find it useful to write a full-length versions of this plan, incorporating references from the text to back up the ideas.

*Show your ideas for staging a performance of* Educating Rita. *Show how you think your ideas would be a good reflection of Russell's intentions.*

Answers to this assignment will vary a lot from one individual to another as it relies on your own ideas. As long as you show your ideas illustrate Russell's themes, you should be rewarded for originality and thought.

- How would you dress the two characters? How would this change? What would Rita wear in the very last scene? Something classic as a statement of her education and rise above the 'class' trap? Or something very casual to signify that she has turned away from snobbish ideas?
- How would Frank's clothing change? Perhaps he would become more and more scruffy and disorganised?
- The set stays more or less the same throughout, but how would you highlight important features like the window, the picture, the bookcase? Would you make any subtle changes to the set, such as to the lighting, placement of objects, tidiness? Why?
- Describe the actress you would cast in the role of Rita. How would you ask her to portray the changes that Rita undergoes in her speech, bearing and movement?
- How would you mark the changing of the seasons during the play? Would you want to mark the passing of time in any other way?
- Pick out a particular scene or section and show how you would direct it to convey Russell's concerns and ideas. Think about expression, movement, voice and pauses in the dialogue. What effect are you trying to achieve?
- Are there any particular aspects of the play that you would like to highlight, for example education, literature, relationships? How would you do this, and why?

You could extend this task by exploring the differences between the restrictions of a staged version of the play and the film of the play.

# The differences between the play scrip

THE PLAY

- All of the dialogue is contained within Frank's study
- We are given information only through the dialogue and stage directions
- Frank and Julia part only when Frank is sent away
- Julia is an ex-student
- We are not told what happens to Denny
- We are not told that Denny is particularly keen on DIY
- Rita does not refer to a sister
- Other students are only referred to
- Rita arrives at Frank's study to talk about his poetry
- Some scenes that appear in the film do not appear in the play
- Rita is told by Frank, in his office, that she has done well in her exams

Can you think of any reasons for thes

## ɪnd the screenplay of *Educating Rita*

THE FILM

- Frank and Rita's scenes switch between Frank's study and the university grounds
- We see scenes of both Rita and Frank's home life, including the introduction of Julia and Denny as characters
- Julia has an affair and leaves Frank
- Julia is described as a 'young tutor'
- Denny meets someone else who becomes pregnant
- Denny's character is depicted as a 'home improvement' fanatic
- Rita has a sister who gets married and is pregnant
- Other students are introduced as proper characters
- Rita arrives at Frank's house to discuss his poetry
- Frank sees Rita off on the train to summer school, and Rita accompanies Frank to the airport at the end of the film
- Rita discovers her exam results at the airport, just before Frank leaves

ɪanges, or what effect they might have?

# Self-test Answers Act 1 Scenes 1–4

**Uncover the plot**

The phone rings and Frank is heard talking to his girlfriend. He is explaining that he will be late because he has to meet his new student. We learn that he has taken on the extra work to pay for his drink. When his student arrives, we find out her name is Susan, although she calls herself Rita after her idol Rita Mae West. Rita picks up a copy of *Howards End* and asks Frank what it is like. Frank says that she can borrow it. We learn from Frank that Rita is a hairdresser. Frank thinks Rita is marvellous. He tells her that he is a bad teacher and refuses to teach her. Rita takes no notice.

Rita returns for her next tutorial and notices that Frank hasn't been drinking. Rita tells Frank that she wants to learn because she wants to change her life. She has read *Howards End* and thinks it is crap. Rita asks Frank about himself and we discover he has split up from his wife. At the next tutorial, Frank is not happy with Rita's essay. At the following meeting, Frank talks about her essay on *Peer Gynt*. Rita has written only one line. She tells Frank that the ideas in the play made her think about the lives of the people around her. Frank makes her do the essay again.

**Who? What? Why? When? Where? How?**

1 Frank's girlfriend, Julia 'phones Frank at the beginning of the play.
2 In Frank's study.
3 To pay for his expensive drinking habit.
4 The handle has not been oiled.
5 She is fed up with her life and wishes to 'discover' herself.
6 She dislikes his attitude towards the poor.
7 He says they split up because of poetry.
8 She used unsuitable reference material (Harold Robbins).
9 'Only connect...'
10 By allowing her to discover the meaning for herself.

**Open quotes**

1 'It's that stupid bleedin' handle on the door. You wanna get it fixed!' Rita, trying to enter Frank's room. Act 1; Scene 1.
2 'There's no suppose about it. Look at those tits.' Rita, looking at the picture on Frank's wall. Act 1; Scene 1.
3 'I don't often consider it actually. I Sometimes get an urge to throw something through it.' Frank, on the window in his study. Act 1; Scene 1.
4 'Soon as I walked in here, I said to meself 'Y' can tell he's a Flora man'.' Rita, on her first impression of Frank. Act 1; Scene 1.
5 'It's a mess. But it's a perfect mess.' Rita, commenting on Frank's room. Act 1; Scene 2
6 'An' it's really temptin' to go out an' get another dress y' know, it is.' Rita, on her reasons for doing the course. Act 1; Scene 2.
7 'And so, to give me something new to write about she left.' Frank, telling Rita why his wife left. Act 1; Scene 2.
8 'What I'd actually like to do is take you by the hand and run out of this room forever.' Frank, talking about the value of education. Act 1; Scene 2.
9 'Possessing a hungry mind is not, in itself, a guarantee of success.' Frank, talking about Rita's inability to concentrate. Act 1; Scene 2.
10 'You go out and buy yourself a new dress and I'll go to the pub.' Frank, when frustrated with Rita's attitude towards Forster. Act 1; Scene 2.

11 'That's justice for y'. I get failed just cos I'm more well read than the friggin' examiner!' Rita, on her essay referring to Harold Robbins. Act 1; Scene 3.
12 'You mean, it's all right to go out an' have a bit of slap an' tickle with the lads as long as you don't go home an' tell your mum?' Rita, re-phrasing Frank's advice on which books to read. Act 1; Scene 3.
13 'You see, a clever answer is not necessarily the correct answer.' Frank, on Rita's short essay. Act 1; Scene 4.
14 'But I don't see any, y' know, culture. I just see everyone pissed, or on the Valium, tryin' to get from one day to the next.' Rita, talking about culture. Act 1; Scene 4.
15 'He hates me comin' here. It's like drug addicts isn't it?' Rita, on her home life and background. Act 1; Scene 4.
16 'If they had the radio in his day that's where he would have done it.' Rita's answer to the *Peer Gynt* question. Act 1; Scene 4.
17 'I could have told you; but you'll have a much better understanding of something if you discover it in your own terms.' Frank, on the phrase 'Only connect...' Act 1; Scene 4.
18 'Y' know Peer Gynt? He was searchin' for the meaning of life wasn't he?' Rita, just before she sits down to rewrite her essay. Act 1; Scene 4.
19 'Right. That's it. I'll never read a Robbins novel again.' Act 1; Scene 3.
20 'I'm dead ignorant y' know.' Rita to Frank, after he has explained the difference between popular fiction and literature. Act 1; Scene 3.

# Self-test Answers Act 1 Scenes 5–8

**Uncover the plot**

Rita is upset because her husband has burnt all her books and her essay. She tells Frank that she must carry on with the course. Frank tries to persuade her to forget the tutorial and go down the pub with him. Rita decides that she wants to go to the theatre. Frank is worried that Julia will be jealous. Frank is taken aback when he realises that Rita wants to see an amateur production.

Rita rushes to see Frank in her lunch hour because she is so excited about the play she has been to see. She has been to see *Macbeth.* As she is about to go back to work, Frank invites her over to his house for dinner.

At the next tutorial, we discover that Rita did not turn up to the dinner party. She let Frank know by posting her essay with a message through his letter box. She explained to Frank that she felt she wouldn't fit in. Afterwards she returned to her family in the pub. Her mother was drunk and started crying for no real reason.

At the next tutorial, Rita turns up with a suitcase. Denny has discovered that she is still on the pill. He told her to forget about the course and stop taking the pill or to leave. She is staying with her mother. Frank tells her that her *Macbeth* essay is moving, but no good for an exam. She is determined to improve.

**Who? What? Why? When? Where? How?**

1 Her husband has burnt them.
2 That she is still taking the pill.
3 Chekhov.
4 Because he felt was trying to create literature.
5 She is excited and wants to tell him about seeing *Macbeth.*
6 Because he wanted her company.

7 Because they could sing better songs.
8 He found out she was on the pill.
9 He doesn't want her to change.
10 She rips it up.

**Open quotes**

1 'Denny found out I was on the pill again; it was my fault, I left me prescription out.' Rita, explaining why her husband burnt her books. Act 1; Scene 5.
2 'You'd think I was havin' a bloody affair the way he behaves.' Rita, on her husbands attitude towards her studying. Act 1; Scene 5.
3 'I've tried to explain to him how you give me room to breathe. Y' just, like feed me without expectin' anythin' in return.' Rita, on her attempt to explain her love of studying to her husband. Act 1; Scene 5.
4 'I said to him, y' soft get, even if I was having an affair there's no point burnin' me books.' Rita, on her argument with her husband. Act 1; Scene 5.
5 'I see him lookin' at me sometimes, an' I know what he's thinking, I do y' know, he's wonderin' where the girl he married has gone to.' Rita, on the breakdown of her relationship with her husband. Act 1; Scene 5.
6 'He thinks we've got choice because we can go into a pub that sells eight different kinds of lager.' Rita, on her husband's attitude to life. Act 1; Scene 5.
7 'He can burn me books an' me papers but if it's all in me head he can't touch it.' Rita, expressing her determination to continue the course. Act 1; Scene 5.
8 'They didn't tell me to stop drinking, they told me to stop displaying the signs.' Frank, explaining why he keeps his alcohol hidden at work. Act 1; Scene 5.
9 'Poets shouldn't believe in literature.' Frank, on why he gave up writing poetry. Act 1; Scene 5.
10 'If she knew I was at the theatre with an irresistible thing like you?' Frank, explaining why Julia wouldn't like Frank going to the theatre with Rita. Act 1; Scene 5.
11 'Life's but a walking shadow, a poor player/that struts and frets his hour upon the stage/And then is heard no more.' Rita reciting from *Macbeth.* Act 1; Scene 6.
12 'Macbeth is flawed by his ambition – yes?' Frank, explaining the nature of tragedy to Rita after she has seen the play *Macbeth.* Act 1; Scene 6.
13 'It's fun, tragedy, isn't it?' Rita, in response to Frank's explanation of tragedy. Act 1; Scene 6.
14 'I can't remember if it's Wilde who's witty an' Shaw who was Shavian or who the hell wrote *Howards End*.' Rita, explaining why she did not go to Frank's dinner party. Act 1; Scene 7.
15 'What's funny? I don't wanna be funny. I wanna talk seriously with the rest of you.' Rita, angry that Frank had invited her to his house to provide some humour. Act 1; Scene 7.
16 'Some stupid woman who gives us all a laugh because she thinks she can learn, because she thinks that one day she'll be like the rest of them, talking seriously, confidently, with knowledge, livin' a civilised life.' Rita, explaining her anger at the reason she was invited to Frank's house. Act 1; Scene 7.
17 'She said, "Because – because we could sing better songs than those".' Rita, telling Frank why her mother was crying in the pub. Act 1; Scene 7.
18 'It's an unashamedly emotional statement about a certain experience.' Frank, explaining why Rita's essay is not good enough to pass an exam, but is impressive anyway. Act 1; Scene 8.
19 '... to pass examinations you're going to have to suppress, perhaps even abandon your uniqueness.' Frank, explaining why he doesn't want to teach Rita to pass exams. Act 1; Scene 8.

20 'If I do somethin' that's crap, I don't want pity, you just tell me, that's crap.' Rita, telling Frank to be strict with her. Act 1; Scene 8.

# Self-test Answers Act 2 Scenes 1–4

**Uncover the plot**

Rita has arrived back from summer school in London. Frank tells her that during his trip to France Julia left him. Rita tells Frank that she has a new flatmate. It is hot weather and Rita is not content to stay in the study. She is disappointed that he is still drinking. Frank wants to introduce Rita to a poet called Blake. He is taken aback when he discovers that she has already covered him at summer school. Rita becomes more friendly with the other students. She seems to have a special interest in one called Tiger. She is pleased when Frank tells her that her last essay is as good as the other students'.

Frank is very drunk when Rita arrives for her next tutorial. Rita suggests that they forget the tutorial. Frank is unhappy with her latest essay because it is not her own opinion. When Rita is late for her next tutorial, Frank 'phones the shop. He discovers that she has changed her job and is working in a bistro. Frank and Rita argue and Frank presents her with his poetry. He asks her to write an assessment of it.

**Who? What? Why? When? Where? How?**

1 She has been to summer school.
2 She has taken on a flatmate, Trish.
3 She has brought him a pen with his name engraved on it.
4 She has adopted a funny voice.
5 He says she is going to fall in love with 'Tiger', or Tyson.
6 He is too drunk to teach properly.
7 He feels it is not her own thoughts and opinions.
8 He has read *Rubyfruit Jungle*.
9 He is upset because she didn't tell him.
10 He asks her to read and assess his own poetry.

**Open quotes**

1 'What are you talking about? London or summer school?' Frank, on Rita's enthusiasm for her trip away. Act 2; Scene 1.
2 'It was right on the tip of my tongue to say "Only when it's served with Parmesan cheese", but, Frank, I didn't.' Rita, telling Frank about talking to a lecturer in the library at summer school. Act 2; Scene 1.
3 'Honest to God, I stood up, an' everyone's looking at me.' Rita, on asking her first question at summer school.
4 'Anyway, the holiday's over, you're back, even Julia's back.' Frank, describing his holiday. Act 2; Scene 1.
5 'Well any analogy will break down eventually.' Rita, defending her comparison of Frank's room to a plant. Act 2; Scene 1.
6 'You will understand Blake; they over complicate him, Rita, but you will understand – you'll love the man.' Frank, on Blake. Act 2; Scene 1.
7 'As Trish says there is not a lot of point in discussing beautiful literature in an ugly voice.' Rita, on her change of voice. Act 2; Scene 2.
8 'For students, they don't half come out with some rubbish y' know.' Rita, on her conversation with some students about the novels of Lawrence. Act 2; Scene 2.

9 'It's all right for them. They *can* just jump into a bleedin' van an' go away. But I can't.' Rita, on her invitation to go to France with the students. Act 2; Scene 2.
10 'To get the sack it'd have to be rape on a grand scale; and not just students either.' Frank, talking about the students' complaint about his drunkenness. Act 2; Scene 3.
11 'Or maybe they did it because they're a crowd of mealy-mouthed pricks who wouldn't know a poet if you beat them around the head with one.' Frank, on the students' complaint. Act 2; Scene 3.
12 'I mean if that poem's only about the blossom then it's not much of a poem, is it?' Rita, arguing about her Blake essay, Act 2; Scene 3.
13 'It struck me that there was a time when you told me everything.' Frank, after finding out that Rita has changed her job. Act 2; Scene 4.
14 ' You really don't have to put in the odd appearance out of sentimentality.' Frank, on Rita's lateness and cancellations. Act 2; Scene 4.
15 'No sentimentality, no subjectivity. Just pure criticism. A critical assessment of a lesser known English poet. Me' Frank, when giving Rita his poetry to assess. Act 2 Scene 4.

# Self-test Answers Act 2 Scenes 5–7

**Uncover the plot**

Rita arrives at Frank's study unexpectedly because she wants to tell Frank that he is a brilliant poet. Frank compares what he has done to Rita to a novel called *Frankenstein.* Rita scornfully tells him that she no longer uses the name 'Rita'. Despite having quarrelled, Frank still phones Rita to tell her when her exam is. When they next meet, Frank is packing to go to Australia. Rita has sat her exam and done well. She has come to thank Frank for being a good teacher. Frank asks Rita to go with him. Rita says that she doesn't know what she will do, but whatever it is, she will choose for herself. Frank gives Rita a new dress. Rita then gives Frank a haircut.

**Who? What? Why? When? Where? How?**

1 She arrives to tell him that his poetry is brilliant.
2 She arrives to tell him he is a good teacher and to thank him for putting her in for the exam.
3 She says that changing her name to Rita was 'pretentious crap.'
4 He phones her to tell her that he has entered her for the exam.
5 Australia.
6 The question on *Peer Gynt* that Frank gave her when she started the course.
7 Her flatmate tried to commit suicide, even though she had everything that Rita wanted.
8 The best thing he has given her is choice.
9 He asks her to go to Australia with him.
10 She gives him a haircut.

**Open quotes**

1 'If you mean am I still this side of reasonable comprehension, then yes.' Frank, when asked by Rita if he is sober. Act 2; Scene 5.
2 'Oh, I've done a fine job on you, haven't I?' Frank, referring to Rita's education. Act 2; Scene 5.

3 '... from now on I shall insist on being known as Mary, Mary Shelley – do you understand that allusion?' Frank, comparing his work on Rita to that of Dr Frankenstein's. Act 2; Scene 5.
4 'You'll find more wit in the telephone book, and, probably, more insight.' Frank, on his own poetry. Act 2; Scene 5.
5 'Found a better song to sing, have you? No – you've found a different song, that's all – and on your lips it's shrill and hollow and tuneless.' Frank, talking about Rita's new-found 'culture.' Act 2; Scene 5.
6 'You stupid... nobody calls me Rita,' Rita, telling Frank that she has changed her name back to Susan. Act 2; Scene 5.
7 'It's like Trish, y' know, me flatmate, I thought she was so cool and together – I came home the other night an' she'd tried to top herself.' Rita, telling Frank that she realises her mistakes. Act 2; Scene 7.
8 'It'd be good for us to leave a place that's just finishing for one that's just beginning.' Frank, asking Rita to accompany him to Australia. Act 2; Scene 7.
9 'I'll make a decision, I'll choose.' Rita, on what she will do next. Act 2; Scene 7.
10 'I'm gonna take ten years off you...' Rita, about to give Frank a haircut. Act 2; Scene 7.

# Notes